Deep River

WALLY METTS

ACCENT BOOKS
Denver, Colorado

ecpa MEMBER OF
EVANGELICAL CHRISTIAN
PUBLISHERS ASSOCIATION

ACCENT BOOKS
A division of Accent-B/P Publications, Inc.
12100 W. Sixth Avenue
P.O. Box 15337
Denver, Colorado 80215

Copyright © 1978 Accent-B/P Publications, Inc.
Printed in the United States of America

All rights reserved. No portion of this book may be reproduced in any form without the written permission of the publishers, with the exception of brief excerpts in magazine reviews.

Library of Congress Catalog Card Number: 78-59936

ISBN 0-89636-008-3

To the Living:
Joan, Wally Jr., Toy, Joy
Mother
Joe, Ronny, Nancy, and Juanita
And in Memory of My Father
Joel A. Metts

Introduction

EVEN IN SOUTH FLORIDA, the cool December air crawled across my bare arms like a fine silk shirt. I stood beneath two scrawny pine trees looking at the fresh grave before me. I was alone for a few minutes and able to do some heavy thinking.

A couple hundred feet away, the Gulf surf was continuing its gentle massage of the white sands of the beach, as even in winter bathers walked about in the brisk air. Sea urchins gathered leaves and moss to camouflage themselves as they rolled in the shallows and fifty brown pelicans stood at attention, every one facing the dying sun in the west from the sandbar that rose a few yards offshore. Life went on.

The body that lay in the grave was that of my father, Joel A. Metts. In many ways he had been a good and decent man. But for thirty of my forty years he had been an alcoholic, and some of the sad scenes of his unfortunate life pushed themselves into my thoughts as I tried soberly to evaluate a lifetime in a few mere minutes.

In the face of death, the dam holding back all the thoughts of the past breaks, and the swelling river of deep

INTRODUCTION

impression begins to overflow the banks of the memory. There are always good times, terrible times and merely usual times in a person's life, and they all played with my thoughts in those moments of reflection.

But the most evident thing I felt even in a time like this, was the unfolding of a purpose, a divine plan that was making its way unerringly toward its destination of glory and destiny. There were bends in the deep river of grace, to be sure, and rapids along the way as it made its way across the path of jagged brown rocks that lie in its path. But I could not help thinking that all along the way it shimmered with its reflection of the One who does all things well.

I bear absolutely no bitterness toward my beloved father. If the portraying of what an unspeakable evil has done to him and those around him will help someone avoid the snares into which he fell, then it will be a fitting memorial to his life.

> All the rivers run into the sea;
> yet the sea is not full; unto the
> place from whence the rivers come,
> thither they return again.
> Ecclesiastes 1:7

Chapter One

THE HALIFAX RIVER runs wide and beautiful by the little town of Port Orange, Florida, where I grew up.

But it is a treacherous river, especially for the inexperienced boatman. Scores of sandbars and mangrove islands provide traps in which the fast falling tide can leave you stranded. There were many times when, as a boy, I pushed or carried a skiff across what seemed like miles of shallow water. I cut my bare feet on the oyster shells at the beginning of the warm weather, but as summer wore on a thick coating of toughened skin gave me feet of armor.

My dog Bill used to get all excited when our little skiff would come near Pelican Island at dusk. But his frantic barking didn't seem to bother the pelicans native to the island at all. I used to wonder at the mystery of this island. Every day at dusk, hundreds of the big brown birds would descend to roost on the small island, ringed with a sandy fringe that separated the river water from the thick grove of mangrove trees where the pelicans spent the night. But you could get there early in the morning and not find anything but their feathers and droppings. I always wondered where they spent the day, and who taught them to congregate together on that one island.

The Halifax separates the mainland of Daytona Beach, five miles to the north of Port Orange, from the beach side. Beyond the peninsula, on the east, lies the Atlantic Ocean. For thirty miles, a wide beach provides tourists with unexcelled bathing pleasure. The sandy shore is three hundred yards wide at low tide and packed hard enough to drive on. We boys, born to mischief, used to row our boats across the Halifax, wade through the tough palmetto plants and sneak into the races at the now-famous Daytona Beach International Speedway. Things were tough in the thirties. We could not have afforded a ticket if we wanted to.

My Dad made out as well as anyone, because he was a hard worker and was endowed with three generations of carpentry know-how. But people didn't build that many houses in those days. While the nation recuperated from the Great Depression, he found what odd jobs he could, planted a garden, and spent the nights firefishing. Some of my fondest recollections of his life are of nights on the Halifax.

Firefishing is done with a three-pronged spear with a ten-foot handle, called a "gig" by the natives. A Coleman lantern is mounted on the bow of a shallow-draught skiff to shine into the water. The fisherman uses the handle of his gig to "pole" the boat along through the shallows. The big prize is the flounder, a flat species that buries himself in the sandy river bottom. His outline is easily seen by the wary firefisherman, though, who usually sends him kicking into the bottom of his boat with a deft flip of the gig.

ONE

I would spend the nights sitting on the back seat of the boat, sipping Dad's mud-like coffee to stay awake. Occasionally, I would doze off sitting there, until a sudden lurch of the boat would threaten to dump me overboard as Dad's skilled hands sent the rowboat darting off toward an escaping sergeant or channel bass. It was a dangerous occupation for me. Once, I awoke to find a snake coiled around my cold feet. More than once, Dad would pole his skiff under a dock, giving me a knot on the head.

As the day broke, he would bring his boat ashore and load the catch in his old truck that was fitted with an insulated body, like an icebox. The rest of the day would be spent peddling the load of fish to a regular round of homes, also suffering from the hard times and eager for a food bargain. If there was any time left to the day, he would spend it jacking up somebody's sagging wooden floor or erecting a clothesline.

The few fish he had left would be combined with the vegetables Mother gleaned from her garden, and grits. We ate fish and grits for breakfast, lunch and dinner. I am not complaining, mind you. Even now I can't think of a better treat than fish and grits. The mullet was the staple of the fisherman's diet. This is a vegetarian fish, the only one in the water with a gizzard, like a fowl. It is swift and runs in schools and is not easily caught with hook and line. The ancient castnet, used for millenniums, served the Florida fisherman well. Dad knitted his own.

The larder was graced occasionally with another treat: swamp cabbage. The outdoorsman would use his axe to separate the heart of the cabbage palm from the stubby limbs that surrounded it. With the outer covering removed, the inside of the heart would be boiled with spices and bacon, providing a distinctive taste all its own.

DEEP RIVER

Sunny days, gorgeous surf, mullet, grits, and swamp cabbage—what more could a person ask for? But the old river ran deep and carried with it many aches and pains.

One of the rare encounters I had with Christianity as a child took place by the riverside. A small crowd had gathered there on the bank not too far from our house, and some people were out in the water acting strangely. I remember asking Mother what they were doing.

"They are having a baptizing," she said.

"What is that?"

"Well, that man out there with them is a preacher. He's dipping them in the water to wash their sins away."

I looked carefully at the flowing river. Even in those days there was a little waste, only we didn't have sense enough to call it "pollution." I saw a few things floating down the river and decided that they were those people's sins. I remember wondering if I had any and if I should have them washed away too.

The only other impression I could remember was when my older brother came home from a tent meeting in town. I had been told that I was too young to go. My brother proudly announced that he had "gone forward" and wanted to be baptized. I thought it was a fine thing that he wanted to wash his sins away, since I could name plenty of them. But my parents apparently thought he was too young to understand, and they dropped the matter right there.

Port Orange Grammar School, as I recollect, didn't have any extracurricular activities except recess, which usually gave the school bullies the opportunity to pick on the other kids. But the main business was learning the main business: reading, writing and arithmetic. It was boring to me. When I was in the third grade I got in trouble with the teacher, who couldn't understand how I

ONE

could sit there drawing pictures all the time. She told me she appreciated the fact that I usually finished my work before the others, but I ought to find something better to do with my time.

Consultations with parents and principal followed until one day she told me she had found a way to get rid of me. She was putting me in the fourth grade in the middle of the year. I remember that the fourth grade teacher was a little more interested in art and more tolerant with my spare time activity. Of course, that made me a little more fair game for the bullies, because I was the youngest and littlest. But I managed to get through those years without too many bumps.

Dad began to act strangely at times during those grade school years, and I didn't understand it. I do remember that I could not see what fascination there was in sitting on a stool in certain public places for hours at a time. Sometimes, especially on weekends, he would turn into a real terror. Since he was gentle and quiet most of the time, I couldn't understand the sudden, violent changes of behavior. I didn't realize at the time what an alcoholic was, nor could I have understood the personality and temperament factors that were changing my Dad into an addict. To the family, those things have a way of dawning slowly.

As the economy improved, Dad's work began to take him to other places. He was developing a recognized brilliance as a builder. My two brothers and I started hanging around construction jobs when we could barely walk. Hammers, saws and two-by-fours were as natural to our lives as breathing.

The country was bracing for the threat of a spreading European war as Hitler marched his troops across the continent. Defense plants were springing up across

DEEP RIVER

America, and knowledgeable builders were in increasing demand. The union wage lured more and more builders into a nomadic life. Our little house in Port Orange was alive with activity one Saturday as we prepared to move south to Riverland, near where Dad was working on a blimp base. Most of the packing was done as we arose early the next day, Sunday, to finish up a few things, load up the old 1935 Ford, and head south. The radio at the end of the hall in the living room was blaring when I awoke, sending out an ominous message difficult for a nine-year-old boy to fully comprehend:

> President Roosevelt has convened an emergency session of congress to consider a formal declaration of war. The Japanese this morning launched a sneak attack on the U.S. military installation at Pearl Harbor, practically destroying our fleet there. . . .

The date, of course, was Sunday, December 7, 1941. And if we had growing apprehension about the drinking habits of our father, we were soon to see the trauma of a great world war tear him apart as it did so many of the nation's men. Before that war ended, we were to see Dad return home from the South Pacific a confirmed alcoholic. It made him one of the innumerable, tragic casualties of that holocaust. And it marred our family's life from that time on.

> Turn again our captivity, O Lord, as
> the streams in the south.
> Psalm 126:4

Chapter Two

THE SAVANNAH RIVER runs blood red in the evening sun, giving the uninitiated observer an eery sense of what Pharaoh must have felt as he stood on the banks of the Nile before Aaron's upraised rod.

Forty miles from where this muddy river passes Augusta, filled with the red clay of Georgia, is the small South Carolina town where I was born. Elko. I have smilingly told audiences that one side of the identification sign says, "Welcome to Elko." The back of the sign says, "Thank you, come back again." I still don't know how few people live in the town that has grown now to two grocery stores, two filling stations and a post office.

Where the road turns off toward Blackwell, past where the old cotton gin used to be, there is the farming section known as Long Branch. It is about two miles out in the country, the sprawling farms reached by centuries-old sand roads. I came forth in a four-room sharecropper's house in which my dad and mother managed the affairs of Grandfather Hair's thousand-acre farm. Grandaddy occupied the respected office of rural mail carrier. He

13

DEEP RIVER

owned a sprawling "modern" home right in town, while his daughter, Lillian, and his son-in-law, Joel, tended the farm. Having left there at the age of six months, I don't remember much about life on the farm.

In the cherished visits to my grandparents' home, I remember the wonderful pecan trees in the backyard where little boys could eat their fill. Out to the side stood the peach trees, the asparagus patch and the standing rows of corn. An ancient old oak tree, fully four feet in diameter, shaded the corner by the side of the road where we used to push our shiny little toy cars through the sand. Outside the kitchen door stood the fearful old well with its drawbucket. I used to have nightmares about falling into that dreadful thing that, to a little boy, seemed like a bottomless pit.

The department store catalog reposed on the shelf of the outdoor facility reserved for a very special purpose. In those days we ate on the inside of the house and went to the bathroom on the outside. Back of the lot—in, behind and on top of the stately, picturesque old barn—we experimented with everything: even flying off the roof with open umbrella. We smoked the "Indian Cigars" that grew strangely on the trees along the fence line, and learned the new "cuss" words.

And oh, that marvelous smokehouse! Every kind of delight in the world released its tantalizing fragrance from that store of plenty. Between Grandmother Hair's smokehouse, pantry and larder, summers in Elko were the highlight of any small child's year.

Uncle Weldon owned and operated the tiny old country "filling station" at the end of the road from Grandfather's house. His big old house was the dwelling of those three wonderful girls who were almost as close as sisters, my double first cousins. That strange kinship had

TWO

been built years before when Weldon had decided to run away and marry Dad's sister, Dottie. Dad and Weldon's sister, Lillian, had decided to make it a foursome. Lillian, my mother, was fourteen at the time.

As the children grew up over the years, we climbed through empty cotton mills, fearfully explored dark country roads, and came home to a country supper and a bath in the galvanized washtub that stayed on the porch or in the kitchen, depending upon the want for privacy. The water bucket, with its common dipper, provided cold, satisfying refreshment. Those seemed to be such happy days.

It was only natural that we would return to that area during the war. After Dad had been drafted and shipped overseas, Mother returned to Elko for awhile and eventually to Augusta, where she worked to keep the family together. In those days, Georgia only had eleven grades in its school system. When I entered the school there, they determined that I was a year ahead of my classmates. I found myself in the seventh grade at the age of ten. I remember how proud I was when Dad showed up in his Navy uniform for my graduation into high school.

Mother worked hard and suffered a great deal to hold things together. By then there were three lively boys and two small girls to care for, besides all the family business. Mother's sacrificial care for us was a great factor in forming our character. And those years provided the opportunity to be near her side of the family and enjoy the rich, rural heritage of that part of the country.

But the Second World War cut loose long-held moral standards for the entire country. Family ties were broken. Roots were torn out, and along with them came the rapid deterioration of the American family. Closely held rural culture became the victim of the cosmopolitan mixture of servicemen from every section of the country.

On weekends, when the GI's drifted into town, merchants vied greedily for their paychecks. Gin mills, flaky nightspots and bawdy houses saturated Broad Street, where we occupied a third story flat. From that dubious vantage, we had the opportunity to learn firsthand every kind of perverted vice that the world had to offer. Fights, open immorality, and roving mobs of teenagers formed the atmosphere of my adolescent years. At eleven, I learned to smoke cigarettes. The age of twelve taught me to gamble. My artistic gift was being exploited by my boyhood friends.

One morning, Mother had gone to work early. It was her custom to get up early without disturbing us, and the clock would be set for me to wake the younger kids and get them started for the day. Mother always started a fire in the fireplace that shared the end of the big bedroom with a closet that contained all our clothing. On this particular morning, I awoke to horror. The whole end of the room was on fire. A spark had apparently ignited a pile of coal on the hearth, turning the whole end of the room into a blaze.

Screaming for help, I carried the younger kids out, then began to remove what furniture I could. By the time the fire department arrived, a neighbor and I had doused the flames.

But every stitch of clothing was gone. The firetrucks and excitement had drawn Mother away from the restaurant, blocks away, to view the disheartening scene. Sadly, after making arrangements for our care, she returned to work and told the people there what had happened. By nightfall, we had a wardrobe twice the size of the original one. The Jewish merchants that frequented the eatery where Mother worked as cashier had brought

TWO

their offerings of new and old goods from their stores. I even owned my first matching suit that day. It made a remarkable impression on me. My curiosity was strangely stirred about these strange people called Jews. And I could never understand after that why so many people hated them. I vaguely recalled how they had something to do with the Bible, and that Jesus was a Jew.

One of my young friends "got religion" and started playing his trumpet on the streets in a stuffy blue uniform. Salvation Army seemed like such a strange name. I liked the lively hymns, and even hummed some of them myself. And occasionally one of my friends would invite me to church. I went a few times and my heart seemed, strangely, to respond to the unusual warmth I felt there. But all the people were so well-dressed and seemed so prosperous. It seemed to me that it was a place for a higher class of people than I could ever hope to be.

The letters we got from New Caledonia in the South Pacific always seemed depressing. Dad was having a lot of trouble with his health. He was in and out of the hospital because of a nervous stomach condition, and he seemed to be all torn up over his absence from the family. Finally, he was released on an honorable discharge. But it seemed to be a different man who came home. I could not fully understand even then what was happening to a nation's families and moral standards. It seemed as if everything was falling apart.

This uncertainty about life was brought home to me quite forcefully as I was walking along Walton Way in Augusta one day. One of my friends, Jock, came running up to me with a piece of news that astonished me.

"President Roosevelt just died."

At first I thought it was a bad joke and I rebuked him

DEEP RIVER

in disbelief. Roosevelt was not a man to a boy like me. He was an institution. Death can happen all around us, but when the head of state dies shockwaves generate to the least of us. Death became a startling reality.

Months later, late at night, lying on a couch at my grandparents' home while Grandfather's body lay in state there, I fell asleep watching the light on Uncle Weldon's service station. Nightmarish, that light came closer and closer. I felt myself being lifted up in the arms of some unknown person or force, and then dropped. There was a terrible sinking sensation of being lowered into a hole in the ground. Fear gripped my heart. I tried to cry out to someone in the house, but the audible sound would not come. Death was haunting my thoughts.

The next day, in a windswept country graveyard, I thought that life must be some kind of cruel joke. The President had died. Grandfather had died. I would die, too. What was there to life but loneliness and death? I was unaware at the time that the awful spectre of death is God's constant reminder of the consequences of sin. I only realized that there was something dreadfully serious that I had not yet caught hold of.

> By the rivers of Babylon, there
> we sat down, yea, we wept, when
> we remembered Zion.
> We hanged our harps upon the
> willows in the midst thereof.
> Psalm 137:1,2

Chapter Three

THE LITTLE BUNGALOW had a front yard that stretched out right into the Halifax River. One night a squall swept in across the river, bringing rains and high wind.

Riding out the storm on the inside, we were startled by a loud crash and strange flapping sounds coming from the front of the house. A huge brown pelican had been swept into the pumping system that pumped the sulphur water from the artesian well into our rented home. He was hurt.

We brought him into the house and nursed him back to health. We tried to make a pet out of him, but our feisty little dog would have no part of this strange intruder. We finally had to release him into the wild habitat of the mangroves.

We had returned to Port Orange after Dad's return from overseas and there we attempted to build a new life. Gathering oysters and clams, casting nets over schools of mullet, and hunting squirrels and swamp cabbage seemed to bring back the happy prewar days.

DEEP RIVER

Victory in Europe came on my birthday, May 8, 1945. A few months later the residents danced in the streets all night when the Japanese surrendered to the allied forces. It is a note that seems missing now from the American scene. It was a note of victory. Hundreds of rolls of bathroom tissue draped across the telephone wires, bands blared in the streets, car horns honked all through the night. The war was won, and a new age had dawned upon planet Earth. The atomic age. The world would never be the same again. But now there was joy in the streets. Our heroes paraded down broad streets to the cheers of thousands. We had fought the war to end all wars and had won.

But it was a costly price we paid. A price exacted not only in human lives, but in fear and uncertainty for a new generation; it was a price exacted in the moral standards of almost two centuries of American traditions of decency, honor and patriotism. We had lost some of that. But we did not fully realize how much we had lost as a family.

Dad's drinking bouts continued to increase. The drugs furnished by government hospitals only made his problem worse. There were very few weekends now when he was sober. We no longer wanted to invite our friends over for fear of being embarrassed. In our high school years, my brother and I hitchhiked to Mainland High School in Daytona Beach. We wore clothes that were too old and too tattered for us, so I went to work. I started out as an usher in a theatre at thirteen, lying about my age. I collected my first paycheck one Friday and lost it the same day in a poker game. Fourteen dollars was a lot of money to go up in smoke, but who cared?

I could get into the pool halls to gamble. I could get into the bars to drink. Daytona was a wild town in those turbulent forties. And the younger set was tasting a new

THREE

liberation. Standards were loosed to the breaking point.

My grades were slipping. Being two years younger than my classmates didn't help that much, either. I was socially retarded, not wanting to go out with girls three grades my junior, but too young for the girls in my grade. There wasn't too much to get excited about in life anyhow. My favorite pastime was just two blocks from school, in the pool hall. Here was something in which I could excel. I practiced before school, during the lunch break and after school before I went to work.

Home became merely a place where we slept at night. Mother was working in a nightspot eatery. One night my brother and I lay awake listening to a familiar sound— arguing parents. There had been a lot of other nights like that, but this one was the culmination of long-standing bitterness. I heard the sickening thud of Dad's hand against Mother's face. That was it. She had had enough. She walked out that night, ending their sixteen-year marriage. Joe and I bathed Dad's head with cold towels through the night and tried to calm him. He begged us to tell him where we had hidden the shotgun so he could blow his brains out.

It is a night that stays before me, even now in my forties. If I had developed any sense of security, any standard by which to measure my life, it seemed swept away with the breaking of the family relationship. Now there was nothing. All my inhibitions melted away. I became a wild thing, as Cain had when he was driven from the farm of his youth. The sky was the limit. Anything that could be done was the thing to do. I added to my patterns of delinquency drinking, cursing, habitual gambling and theft. My brother Joe soon left for the Air Force, and both my parents tried in their way to provide for me, but I was filled with bitterness and mischief.

DEEP RIVER

Athletics was fast becoming the god of academic life, but I was clumsy and slow. I was accident-prone. By the age of twelve, I had had a broken arm, a broken leg, and five fractured ribs. I'd been hit twice by automobiles and saved from drowning three times. Needless to say, I could not excel in sports, although I tried. I could not even keep up with my fast-living peers. I was too immature physically to be adept at their frequent sexcapades, and too poor to keep up with their fast social life. I wandered. From relative to relative and from friend to friend. By the time I graduated I had attended five different high schools and lived in 27 different towns.

The first part of my senior year, at the age of fifteen, found me enrolled in Richmond Military Academy in Augusta, Georgia, living with my aunt. It was an all-boys school with many extremes. I dropped out of chemistry because of an insufficient background. The typing teacher there just handed us a book at the beginning of the year and turned us loose. And the environment did not help me any in the morality department, although there was a structured discipline that I needed.

I left there and started back at Mainland High School in Daytona midway through my senior year. A student activist, I called a strike of the whole senior class to get our senior privileges, recently removed, restored to us. It worked, too. Even then school administrations were beginning to yield to student pressure. The year was 1948.

Graduation was in two weeks. We were standing in line one day, waiting to be fitted for our caps and gowns. The dean came up behind me, tapped me on the shoulder, and firmly informed me that I would not be receiving a diploma, so I might as well get out of line. I had flunked typing.

My heart exploded with bitterness. It was a harsh blow.

THREE

It was fortunate that they were kind enough to give me my grades later, because I never set foot in that school after that day.

Searching for some meaning to life, I developed a peculiar fondness for the Darwinian philosophy. I would gather friends around me in the late hours and preach the latest shades of evolutionary thought to them. They were fascinated with my knowledge. I decided that I was intelligent enough to make it without a high school diploma anyhow. After all, one man's viewpoint is as good as another's. But the hand of Providence was working behind the scenes.

I could not turn down the salary that Dad offered me to come to Stuart, where he had landed a job as superintendent on a huge construction project. It was three times more than I was making in a theatre. I didn't know it at the time, but I'm sure the Lord wanted to move me away from the scene of my educational demise so I would finish high school. I needed the change.

> The beasts of the field cry also unto thee: for the rivers of waters are dried up, and the fire hath devoured the pastures of the wilderness.
> Joel 1:20

Chapter Four

THE ST. LUCIE RIVER connects the eastern waters of Florida with the intercoastal waterway. A retired doctor used to take us young men camping on its banks, where we stalked the wild pig, the bobcat and the Florida panther. He would astound us with wild tales about fishermen being attacked by wildcats. Once, while gathering firewood along one of the St. Lucie's tributaries, I walked within a foot of a coiled rattlesnake. Without a word or a twitch, Dr. Barr slid his Luger pistol out of his belt and shot the snake's head off. He could split a bullet on the blade of a hunting knife at forty paces.

He wasn't that much of a moral influence, although we appreciated someone taking an interest in us. I remember when he tried to introduce us to chewing tobacco. I had done a lot of things, but I couldn't stomach that. After a couple of minutes, I relieved my mouth of its unwelcome burden while the others weren't looking, and went around the rest of the night working my jaws as if I were still chewing the vile stuff.

Stuart was booming in those days, like the rest of the

FOUR

Sunshine State. And I enjoyed the change. Although Dad drank constantly, I thought I could handle it better now. And there was this girl from Daytona. She was pretty, freewheeling, and she had enough Latin blood in her to make her constantly interesting, although she was older than I. We developed a nice friendship, and she helped me not to hate girls anymore. Our relationship was a rather mild one by most standards in those days, and she gave me something of the security I needed in the status of a friend of the opposite sex.

But my rollicking, shameful ways continued. A new dimension was added to my youthful experiments: nightclubbing. I could go into any nightclub in the Fort Pierce, Stuart and Palm Beach area and drink as much as I wanted at the age of 16. I even began to aspire to a career in entertainment, organizing a hopeful but completely hopeless musical group called "Madman Metts and his Musical Maniacs." It flopped, of course, because I have a tin ear. I was pretty fair on the trumpet, but the jazzy music of the forties demanded an ear that I didn't have.

I also struck out in my career as a professional athlete. We had a fairly successful semi-pro football team in town, which I joined. But I spent all my time running errands and sitting on the bench. At 125 pounds, what can you do? It did introduce me to some of the racier set, though, and provided a little more status. There had to be some daring exploits to share with others, so we broke into a few fruit stands for kicks. Nothing came of it, though. I did not even seem capable to mount a serious life of crime.

More money gave me a new freedom and an elevated sense of security. I didn't own a car. Believe it or not, Dad was still driving that 1935 Ford. I was ashamed to go anywhere in it. We went our separate ways. Dad had

DEEP RIVER

already experienced another marriage and subsequent divorce. I couldn't really care less in those days if he wanted to throw his life away.

But Christmas that year found a soft spot in my armor. It came and went like a black shroud. There was no music, no gaiety and no Christmas tree. As soon as Dad got off work for the Christmas break, he began his binge. When Christmas Day dawned, I wandered finally out of my room about nine o'clock. I heard noises in the kitchen. I found Dad there, crouching on the floor in his underwear, unable to stand. He was trying to get some food off the stove. Finally, he pulled a pot of cold grits off the stove, sending it crashing to the floor. He dug his hands into the pot, filling his mouth with cold grits. I walked out in disgust.

I spent that Christmas walking the streets of Stuart. There were a few places open, but when I found one I stopped to sample their coffee. I didn't eat. I was too lost. Across the world, a million other alcoholics' sons probably discovered that their fathers could not even stand the gaiety of the Christmas season, the most significant family day in the year.

It was strange that, in the midst of all this, I should have the motivation to go back and finish high school. The job finished up in January and Dad left for another location. I guess there wasn't anything else to do, so I signed up for band, journalism and Latin American History at the beginning of the second semester in Martin County High School.

It was a fun time. I loved journalism, even winning a national essay contest. My journalism teacher tried to encourage me to make that my career choice, but I didn't really want to think about a career. I was also the artist for *The Southwind,* the school paper.

FOUR

The river of grace was flowing in the halls of that school, though. My younger brother, Ronnie, had stayed with Dad and me briefly there in Stuart. One day, a couple who were "going steady" approached me in the hall. I was fascinated by a strange, happy glow that shone from their faces.

"Did you know that your brother was saved before he left?"

"He was what?"

"He was saved. We got the request for his membership to go to the church in Naples where he is attending now."

"That's, uh . . . nice." I didn't know anything else to say.

But I was struck by their countenances. They had a reputation for being nice kids, but they sure didn't fit in with my crowd. I pondered briefly what it meant to be saved before I tucked the whole incident away somewhere in the back of my mind. Still, the thought occasionally lingered of some kind of strange quality I couldn't put my finger on.

Graduation came in June, just after I turned seventeen. I had been staying with a kind family who had taken me in for the balance of the school year. They were proud of me, and the crowd there seemed to applaud a little louder when I received my high school diploma, but none of my family was there. I guess by that time it didn't matter much. At midnight that night, I boarded a Greyhound bus with Nick, a much older friend, bound for Philadelphia and a new life of adventure.

The gang I joined on the streets of the big city consisted of thirteen members, all of them in their twenties. At last, I became a bigtime sinner. All-night beer parties, drugs, street fights, thefts—the works. Everything was falling into place for me except my retarded relationship with the opposite sex. But I didn't fit in too well with the Yankee environment. They kept calling me "farmer" because I was from the South.

There weren't any jobs to be had. Nick and I subsisted on loans, handouts, and early morning forays that lifted doughnuts and milk from the doorways of unsuspecting neighbors. We had plenty of time for mischief. One morning, well past midnight, we were standing on the street corner, all thirteen of us, throwing objects at passersby and hurling appropriate epithets at those who were unfortunate enough to talk back.

I was still trying to get something going with a girl, and when a cute little blonde walked by that I had met, I graciously offered to walk her home, as any southern gentleman would. We had only walked a few steps down the street when I saw the reflection of flashing red lights in a store window. We turned to see what was upon us in time to see all twelve of my gang being hauled into a police van. They were arrested for corner lounging and disturbing the peace. It fell my lot to contact the local alderman, well known to some of the gang, and arrange to get them out. But not until they had taken back some of that stuff about ignorant farmers from the South.

I had lost about twenty pounds and my patience was wearing thin. One night in our room, Nick and I had it out in a bloody fistfight. He was older and stronger, of course, and got the best of me easily. That ended my fascination for big city life. I drifted back to Augusta to visit Mother for a short time, and then hitchhiked south to Naples, Florida. The river of grace began to run swifter now, as the relentless seeker of men hounded my faltering steps. It was September, 1949.

> There is a river, the streams whereof shall make glad the city of God, the holy place of the tabernacles of the most High.
> Psalm 46:4

Chapter Five

IT IS ONE of the most unusual rivers in the world. The Seminoles called it "the river of grass." Flowing from Lake Okeechobee, the second largest inland lake in America, this vast river flows across miles of marshland in a wide sweep. The alligator, the otter and the heron share this natural marsh river with thousands of other varieties of wildlife. Hunters stalk the tiny key deer and the wild hog in its thousands of cypress heads, where wild turkey roost at night.

Occasionally, a patch of palmettos or pines rises above its fruitful waters, called "islands." The thousands of square wilderness miles of this last of America's frontiers gave rise to what may be one of the most unusual do-it-yourself hobbies in the world, the swamp buggy. The old Model A Fords used to make it pretty well through the woods and marshes of the Everglades, but running them constantly in low gear heated up the transmissions and left early pioneers stranded in the forbidding swamps.

One of the early woodsmen, eager to penetrate deeper into the "glades," got the idea of taking old tire carcasses big enough to cover the ones mounted on his Ford, cutting chunks out of them, and using them to gain more traction. It is said that Firestone, out with one of the colorful Everglades guides for a hunting trip, took the idea back to his plant and introduced the lug grip tire to the world. Around Naples, Everglades City, Fort Myers and Bonita Springs, local enthusiasts built swamp buggies of every conceivable design and shape. After World War Two, surplus bomber tires began to appear on the strange looking vehicles. Mounted on light chassis with four-cylinder engines, the buggies would actually float across a pond, the drive wheels acting as paddle wheels.

It was drizzling rain when I caught ride number eleven that finally took me to the four corners in Naples. It was daybreak. No more than four thousand people lived in the Naples area at that time, most of them winter residents. Millionaires were plentiful. Briggs of engine fame, Fleischmann of the yeast empire and Lester Norris, then owner of the controlling share of Texas Oil Company were just a few of the wealthy that wintered in this tropical paradise.

A local newspaper carrier was able to tell me where J. A. Metts lived, and I soon found myself knocking on the dilapidated screen door of a little white frame house. Dad appeared at the door drunk at six-thirty in the morning, but I wasn't shocked. We chatted awhile. I asked about Ronnie. He told me about Ronnie's girlfriend, the daughter of one of the town's most prosperous merchants. They lived in the gold coast section, and Dad was proud of his son's new status. But he had a warning for me.

"She has a sister that you don't want to get mixed up with. She's a real nitwit."

I was mildly curious. When my brother arose to get

FIVE

ready for school, he made a point of insisting that I meet his girl. We made a date to meet after he got out of school that day. After breakfast, Dad took me out to a local tavern on the outskirts of town, bought me a few beers while he filled me in on the townspeople and matched me with the local pool sharks.

I was impressed with the big, breezy house on Seventh Avenue. Although its gorgeous surroundings spoke of affluence beneath the surrounding coconut trees that stretched to the nearby Gulf of Mexico, the house looked comfortable and betrayed the casual lifestyle of Southwest Florida. Betty, Ronnie's girl, was very friendly and made me feel at home. It was kind of odd, though, because he was only fourteen at the time and she was eighteen.

As we stood in the front yard, enjoying the wonderful tropical air and unfailing sunshine, two teenagers walked up the street toward the house. They were dressed almost identically, although one was a boy and the other was a girl. The girl wore a Boy Scout shirt, shirttail out, and jeans rolled up, one higher than the other. Her honey-blonde hair fit the gentle Gulf breeze, and her gait was free and casual.

"Here it comes; let's go in the house," Betty said.

"Here comes what?" I asked, puzzled.

"My little sister," she said with a trace of impatience.

Joan's entrance into the living room was with fanfare. She didn't just walk in, she buzzed in.

"Don't tell me you're his brother," she said.

I confessed, somewhat reluctantly, that I was.

After excusing herself, she appeared a few minutes later dressed more appropriately for company. She was charming. I felt drawn to her winsome way immediately. And there was that quality again. That indescribable

DEEP RIVER

something that I had sensed once before, when those two teenagers approached me in the hall at Martin County High School.

A few nights later, Joan and I had our first outing that could be called a "date." I didn't have a car. We walked several blocks to the drugstore, had a hot dog and Coke, and walked back to her house along those enchantingly beautiful palm-lined streets that caught the glow of the tropical moon. I was enjoying myself to the hilt, and we were just walking and talking!

I liked this girl. I knew that an experienced, worldly fellow like myself would have no trouble sweeping such a small-town girl off her feet, and I got down to business right away, although I was really clumsy at this sort of thing. In her front yard, beneath the incredible beauty of those towering palms, I cupped my hands about the sides of her lovely face.

"Do you know what I usually do to girls when I get them like this?" I asked in my best Valentino.

"What?"

"I usually kiss them."

The setting was perfect, and my heart was pounding. Suddenly I felt a sharp pain in my stomach. She had let me have it right in the breadbasket. When I was finally able to straighten up, she was standing on the front porch of her house.

"Not this girl," she said just before she disappeared into the house.

The biggest shock was yet to come. The little blow to the stomach did not compare with the blow that was soon to be delivered. I had scraped up the money for an old car, and Joan reluctantly consented to a few more dates. She had, of course, shown me exactly where she stood.

As I recall, we were talking about our families, as kids

FIVE

sometimes do when they are getting acquainted. I don't know why I was able to open up and unburden my heart, but somehow she had gained my confidence and penetrated the hard surface I had put up to protect myself from more hurt. I told her how I felt about a drunk father, a broken home and all the rest.

I felt foolish when she told me of an incident in her life that overshadowed anything that had ever happened to me. Nine years before, on a Sunday morning, her mother had started off to the Methodist Sunday School in the family pickup. At the corner of Fifth Avenue and Third Street there was a grinding, tragic crash. Joan's mother died at the scene. Her three-year-old brother, John, suffered injuries that left him mentally handicapped. Her other two sisters were not badly hurt, but Joan was left partially blind, with an eye hanging from its socket, and serious head injuries. Unconscious for days, with the grieving family uncertain of her fate, Joan was thought soon to be buried with her mother, whose funeral was delayed for a time to await the outcome.

I sat meekly listening to her as she told me of the accident, of her mother's death, and of the multiple tragedies set in motion by that missing mother. And then came the bombshell. Calmly, with perfect assurance, she said, "But I know I'll see my mother again."

"How can that be? How can you know a thing like that?"

"I know I'll see her again because she was a Christian. I know she's in Heaven, and that's where I'm going, so I'll see her again someday."

She said it so calmly, so matter-of-factly. Somehow, a wonderful, unseen reality began to dawn upon my dark mind. Here was a person who talked about another world. Not just about church, or religion, or how to

DEEP RIVER

behave, but about living again—about living forever. It was almost too much.

"Do you know what you need?" she asked.

"What?"

"You need a Friend."

"Yeah, I do. You'll be my friend, too. I appreciate what you're saying, although I don't understand."

"I'm not talking about me. 'There is a friend that sticketh closer than a brother'; and His name is Jesus."

There is no doubt that the Heavenly Shepherd, seeking His lost sheep, put those words in her mouth. He knew exactly what I needed. If there was anything in the world that was a real need in my life, it was a true friend. Those ten words exploded in my heart: "There is a friend that sticketh closer than a brother."

Joan told of how she used to climb up into the coconut tree behind her house and read a tiny little Gideon New Testament, finally being conquered by the beatitudes:

> Blessed are the poor in spirit: for theirs is the kingdom of heaven.
> Blessed are they that mourn: for they shall be comforted.
> Blessed are the meek: for they shall inherit the earth.
> Blessed are they which do hunger and thirst after righteousness: for they shall be filled.
> Blessed are the merciful: for they shall obtain mercy.
> Blessed are the pure in heart: for they shall see God.
>
> Matthew 5:3-8

She then told me of how, at the age of ten, walking

FIVE

along the shore of the Gulf of Mexico, she invited the Friend of friends into her heart.

A living God? Could it be? This Jesus, this One Who died, was it possible that He was alive? It was incredible. And yet, there was no argument for the astonishing reality in this girl's life. Something was there.

I began to attend church with Joan, my lovely angel of good news.

It was on a Sunday night. I had heard the congregation sing the old sing:

> There is a fountain, filled with blood,
>   Drawn from Immanuel's veins;
> And sinners, plunged beneath that flood,
>   Lose all their guilty stains.

The age-old gospel sounded forth from the pulpit of that little church, as I suddenly came to realize that all the rivers in the world cannot wash away a single sin. Only one thing can do that. The blood that was shed for sinners by the mighty, conquering, virgin-born Son of the living God. And yes, now He lives, Victor over the grave. My heart went out to Him that night. He had conquered again.

As I went forward in public testimony that I had invited Christ into my life, that word I had heard in the hall of the high school months before rang through my heart. Saved!

I looked for a face in the crowd. I looked until I saw the face of the charming instrument that God had used to reach me. Joan stood sheepishly back with a shining face, her eyes brimming with tears. Now I know that they both had conquered my heart.

> And the daughter of Pharaoh
> came down to wash herself at the
> river; and her maidens walked
> along by the river's side . . .
> Exodus 2:5

Chapter Six

JACK PRINCE was a born entrepreneur. In the late twenties he had discovered the tropical paradise on the lower west coast of the state where Joan grew up.

Naples was very tiny then, the first town one comes to in Florida's largest county. Named Collier County after the pioneering railroad magnate, Barron Collier, most of it was made up of the Everglades swamplands. These slow-moving fresh waters overflowed from Lake Okeechobee and its rich bottom lands to flow in a wide, shallow stream southward to the Big Cypress and other giant swamps in Collier and Lee County. South of Naples, tiny little Everglades City was the county seat. It was between there and Miami that the vast river marshes emptied their brackish water into the endless green jewels offshore and in back bays called the Ten Thousand Islands.

A group of wealthy Kentuckians had discovered the beauty of Naples-On-The-Gulf. There were no roads to span the Everglades, so early settlers built a long pier out into the gulf waters where supplies could be brought in

SIX

for their buildings. Still there, replaced after numerous hurricanes, the thousand-foot fishing pier is an attraction to the growing tourist trade in the town.

A gunnery school had located in Naples during the Second World War, and servicemen stationed there were captivated by the natural beauty and the ideal year-round climate. Many of them returned to settle there after the war, a movement that did not go unresisted by the wealthy who had enjoyed the unspoiled beauty with only a few local Florida Crackers to share it with. The town boomed. The year I arrived there, 1949, it was listed as one of the fastest growing communities in the United States.

But Jack Prince had arrived long before that. Fresh from the western oilfields, this young man became a part of the local Naples scene, buying property and going into various businesses. For a long while, he operated the town drugstore, a distinction that earned him the title, "Doc." The property around Naples was dirt cheap. Lots could be bought for twenty dollars apiece. Jack Prince bought up the local property with a shrewdness that soon made him wealthy.

The spirit of the western prospector was still in his veins, so Jack roamed the state in search of new adventure. Supplies had to be bought for his grocery store from a distance, necessitating frequent trips north to the supply port at Tampa. Joan looked forward to these trips with her dad, especially when they would visit the Columbia Restaurant in Ybor City for a tasty Cuban sandwich. During these journeys, Jack Prince developed a love for treasure hunting, a hobby which he pursued for years with success.

He had a little device with which there was an uncanny ability to locate lost objects. I could never understand ex-

DEEP RIVER

actly how it worked, but it was a procedure akin to water-witching. The local people would spin yarns about how detectives, federal agencies and others would use his services in locating stolen loot and missing bodies.

It was a quiet, undisturbed town of unparalleled beauty that nurtured Joan in those early years. Life was made up of quiet walks through the woods, fishing, alligator hunting and barrels of fresh air and sunshine everywhere she and her young companions turned. The rich luxury of fabulously beautiful beach homes were theirs to enjoy during the summers when the wealthy were in the North and local friends took care of their homes and yards.

Shoes were forbidden in the summer, except for church. Naples young people were like South Sea natives, tanned, casual and tough. Joan could open a coconut in three minutes flat with her bare hands and feet.

They grew up like fish, sharing the gentle surf of the gulf with the friendly porpoises and gliding brown pelicans. You can practically swim year-round in that place, and they have three vegetable crops every year. The profusion of tropical life was everywhere. Oranges, grapefruit, tangerines and guavas graced the trees. Mangos, papayas, berries and other juicy treats hung everywhere, adding to the abundance of fresh game and fish. It would be very difficult to starve to death there.

In the early thirties, Jack became the proprietor of The Flamingo Grill, a lonely outpost that stood like a vigil on the edge of Naples where the Tamiami Trail turned sharply to the east. This picturesque road had been built across the hundred and a half miles of swamplands from Fort Myers to Miami at a great cost of men and materials. Without the huge earth-moving equipment of today, it was a difficult engineering feat to span the Glades in those days. A huge, cumbersome piece of equipment

SIX

called "the walking dredge" had been used to cross the marl pits and forbidding gator holes. The heat, the snakes and the mosquitoes took a heavy toll before the road was finally completed. When done, it was the only land link connecting Tampa and Miami, two Florida cities fast growing in importance.

Thirsty, tired travelers welcomed a place at the halfway mark, and the grill became famous for its strategic location. Thomas Edison, Al Capone, The Prince of Wales, and a couple of presidents were among the important people who paused there for meals and refreshment. While barefooted, brown-skinned children romped about, Jack would amuse his infrequent guests with wild tales of his treasure hunting and prospecting.

After the tragic crash that took the life of her mother, Joan suffered no small amount of emotional upheaval. Her dad was never the same, although he married again soon. A stern old housekeeper raised the kids, locking them in closets for punishment, scaring them with stories of how "the devil is going to get you," and giving them massive doses of Milk of Magnesia every time they became the least bit ill. They soon learned not to become ill. Old-timers cured a lot of imaginary ills ahead of time with Black Draught, castor oil and Milk of Magnesia. It was good preventive therapy that might bear repeating in our neurotic, sick age.

John, Joan's brother, was soon placed in an institution in which he could be properly cared for. Her two older sisters seemed, on the surface, to adjust better than she did. Joan withdrew, taking hours to think and meditate upon the meaning of life and all its mysteries. She had difficulty with her school work, but not because of a lack of intelligence. It was more of an emotional withdrawal. Her dad, concerned, commented frequently on her apparent lack of mental ability, leaving a deep impression on her mind.

With great difficulty in communicating with others, she put on the witty, flighty mask of humor and cheer that caused my dad to call her a nitwit. Actually, she was crazy like a fox. She had a scary, penetrating perception about people. Hesitant to place her confidence in anyone, she stood aloof and sized them up with ocean-deep philosophies anchored to nature, tragedy and her Gideon New Testament. I still turn her radar loose on people about whom I need some valid information.

They went to Sunday School every Lord's Day at the Methodist Church. After the accident, Jack became disillusioned about the church and opened up a liquor store to replace his grocery business at the four corners. When I arrived in Naples, he had the largest liquor store there and owned much of the commercial property around the four corners, as well as a farm on Shell Island Road, thirteen miles to the south. Already bitter about the effects of alcohol, I developed a growing resentment against the Prince family business.

But I sure liked one of the Prince products. Joan was the most charming, the most mysterious, the most wonderful troublemaker I had ever met. And, of course, after my decision to receive Jesus Christ I felt I owed her my life.

I made the mistake of telling her early in our relationship that I was in love. We dated often, developing a relationship punctuated by the breakups and makeups that are so characteristic of young lovers. For a long time, I didn't even know if I was in the running. Her depth of personality, beauty and winning sense of humor attracted a large male following. And she was possessed of a beautiful soprano singing voice. She served the Lord the

SIX

best she could, singing, witnessing and inviting friends to church. Wally Beebe, the nationally-famous Sunday School bus expert, first heard the gospel in Naples at her prodding. His father operated the Beach Club, a fashionable hotel on the golf course. Wally and I were both unconverted when we first met in the Prince's front yard.

When it is all written in eternity's record book, there will probably be some surprises. For one thing, a small town girl, saddened by the loss of her mother, converted on a lonely beach, faithful to witness when she could, will share mightily in the rewards of a couple of teenage boys who, influenced by her faithful witness, later went on to preach the gospel of Jesus Christ across the nation. It pays to be faithful. The river of God's grace takes strange, unexpected turns as it runs along its appointed path.

> "... and from the city that is
> by the river ... the Lord our God
> delivered all unto us ..."
> Deuteronomy 2:36

Chapter Seven

HORSE CREEK drains the swamps around roots of the red mangrove to where it dumps its tannin-saturated waters into Gordon River. The roots of this important tree reach across mud and sand flats like some kind of great insect. Below the murky waters, mussels and other marine life feed on its rich nutrients. Biologists say that the red mangrove is the vital link in the Everglades food chain. From the brown crust on its leaves caused by feasting bacteria and fungi, the deteriorating leaf eventually falls in particles to rest in the swirling current mixed with the mud of the bottom. A young striped mullet will scoop up the mud, filtering out the vegetable matter for his diet before a speedy snook will nab the unwary mullet for his own dinner.

The profuse marine life of the area is a living picture of the abundant life I found in Jesus Christ. But that life takes place against the background of much adventure and testing.

Being a Christian was a wonderful thing, even when heartaches came along. New converts didn't come along

SEVEN

every day in the week in that little town. I soon found that the church offered plenty of opportunities to serve. I started taking up the offering in church. Then I was given the job of songleader. As I look back, I think they very well may have been desperate. I taught Sunday School, did carpenter work on the building and even preached.

Not too long after I came into this new life, the preacher was going to be out of town for a Sunday and wanted me to speak. I have no idea why. I stumbled and faltered through that first talk. The people seemed to enjoy it, but I was a nervous wreck.

Not too long after that, he asked me to do it again. To my utter shock, three teenagers came to the front of the church desiring to know the Saviour about whom I had tried to talk. I didn't know what to do with them. I prayed with them the best I could. A lot of the folks around the church tried to call me into the ministry then, and I thought about it. But I also had another goal, overcoming poverty. I was ashamed of being poor. My folks had owned only one home in my entire life, a little bungalow that they paid on during the depression. I looked around at all the fine homes and longed for something more.

The swamp buggy owners had been racing with one another in the Everglades to test the relative efficiency of their rigs. Somebody got the idea of making the races into an annual "event," and the first Swamp Buggy Days was born November, 1949, with great hoopla.

It was going to be advertised, organized and done in such a way as to put tiny little Naples on the map. An "advertising man," a character who had sold himself to the city fathers, was to be the promoter for this first big event. That meant that he would try to get something printed and find somebody to do the posters and signs to

DEEP RIVER

be draped across the Tamiami Trail. He got wind of the fact that a new kid in town had some drawing talent, and my advertising career was born.

I didn't know anything about making posters and signs, but he assured me that anybody who could draw pictures could surely paint signs. It sounded reasonable. I worked hard on those signs. It was going to be a big event, complete with a rolling jail for men who refused to grow beards, banquets and balls, a parade, and the choice of some attractive young lady to earn the dubious title, "Swamp Buggy Queen." She was later ceremoniously dumped into the three foot layer of soft mud that comprised the mile long track on Radio Road.

The promoter was supposed to meet me at the parade on Saturday to pay me the money he owed me. I haven't seen him to this day. But the introduction to the sign business was begun, continuing for nine years. I drove nails in the daytime and painted signs, posters and pictures at night. That beginning eventually led to the largest outdoor advertising business in the fastest-growing county in the United States.

After my conversion, my desires changed sharply. I no longer drank, swore or gambled. It took awhile, however, to build some convictions about the kind of places a Christian ought to go. When a hillbilly band came to town and announced a square dance every Saturday night in the American Legion hall, Joan and I thought we would join in the fun.

It was a brawl. While the promoters could not sell alcoholic beverages, those who came were invited to bring their own. Young teenagers stumbled around the place, thoroughly drunk. My newly-changed conscience was fully aroused. Joan and I left soon after we got there, but when I got home I could not sleep. Very late, with a burn-

SEVEN

ing heart, I got up from my bed and began a letter to the editor of *The Collier County News.* I no longer have a copy, but I remember the way it started:

> A long, snakelike mass of fun-crazed human beings twisted, kicked and staggered their way through the final stages of a square dance. People fell to the floor, passing out in the middle of a dance. Over in one corner, a whiskey-mad youth cursed as he floundered on the floor. . . .

My pen wrote furiously (remember, I had flunked typing!). Whatever else I said in that letter, I know I couldn't rest until I got it said. Before I went to bed, I put a stamp on it and took it out to the mailbox.

It probably would go little noticed now, but in those days a community still had something of a conscience. Adult indignation hit a high pitch, and the town talked. Two weeks later, the dance had to close up for lack of customers. A friend of mine told me that the band had laid in wait for me the last night, but they somehow missed me. I had discovered the power of words, and I would never be the same again.

A young man named Ted Yates was the sports editor for that little weekly paper. He was moving to New York to go into big time journalism, later going on to write for *David Brinkley's Journal.* He was finally killed while covering the Six Day War in Israel. When he left Naples, the editor called me and asked me if I would like to work for the newspaper on a space rate basis. I excitedly took him up on the offer. Most of the sports news in those days had to do with fishing. I was not much of an expert on angling. Most of my fishing had been done with gigs and nets. But I tried. The editor had to work with me, though, because I had this urge to preach through my column, "Along the Gulf." It is hard to moralize about fish.

At the age of nineteen, I was writing my weekly column, working as a carpenter foreman, painting signs in my spare time, attending to my church duties and courting Joan. Opportunities as a lay preacher kept coming up, too. I spoke to my pastor about the call to preach, but he discouraged me.

Joan seemed to have increasing trouble at home. We know now that many of the things we thought were troublesome at home were of our own invention. But we prayed together about those things and kept on trying to serve the Lord. I had organized a youth choir in the church that sang on the radio once each month. We were attracting increasing numbers of young people into the church. Seeing the need to do something for alcoholics in the area, I helped organize a local chapter of Alcoholics Anonymous in the church fellowship hall. But Joan's troubles with her parents seemed to get worse.

One day I rode back from the construction site in Bonita Springs, a few miles north, with the car pool. Joan met me at the city limits in my 1941 Chrysler which I had loaned her for the day. When I walked over, she said very calmly, "Let's go get married."

That's a nice greeting. We had planned our wedding for a few months hence when she would be eighteen. I had wanted to marry her for two years, but facing the actual fact was something else. Something had happened to hurt her deeply that day, something that I still do not fully know about.

"Let's not be so hasty," I protested.

"If you don't marry me, I know someone who will!"

I could tell she wasn't joking. I drove to the store to see

SEVEN

her dad. Surely, something could be worked out. He told me, correctly, that we were too young to get married. He told me that our relationship was hurting Joan's chances to finish school. It was true. She was making a choice between her family and me, and it was not fair to them. He told me that the best thing for me to do was to leave town until she was a little older. He didn't have anything against me personally.

We were foolish kids. I did leave town, thirty minutes later. With his daughter. We had gone to the church, bowing together before the pulpit in an empty building, asking the Lord to help a couple of foolish and scared young people. As we crossed the county line, I prayed again, something like this, "Lord, if you don't want us to do this, stop us now. Let something happen to stop us."

I prayed it aloud as Joan cried on my shoulder. That old Chrysler just kept going, with its bald tires and ten-year-old body breezing north toward Tifton, Georgia. I'm not too sure that such a prayer is the best way to test the will of the Lord. But He permitted us to go anyhow.

Across the border, we were unable to get married because of Joan's age. We decided to drive to Augusta, where my mother was. In order to keep her dad from worrying, we wired him to inform him of our intention. We were running scared.

As it turned out, we had quite a wedding party. Mother, my sisters, my brother Ronnie, my cousin, my grandmother and a few others attended our wedding in Aiken, South Carolina. I would have preferred a church wedding. But I meant it when I spoke those vows to that judge, repeating them before he had a chance to rehearse them to me. Before we got back to Augusta, just minutes away, the generator burned out in that old car. I pushed it down Broad Street in Augusta, tin cans clanging along

DEEP RIVER

the street. We had hamburgers for our wedding supper, and spent our first night in a dumpy little tourist court south of town.

I don't know if it is any indication of anything, but in addition to the trouble with the generator, we had five flat tires on the way back to Florida. Those tires were really slick. It was a minor miracle that we had gotten to our wedding place.

I am so thankful that the Lord brought us together. Joan was not only the instrument to bring me to Christ, but she has been a sustaining force from that day. She complements my weaknesses. She understands my needs. She loves me. We started our lives together in a tourist cottage on the outskirts of Naples, and it has been a honeymoon most of the time since.

But in our foolish haste we had hurt some people that we loved. Her father was hurt deeply. He ordered her out of the house, pronounced her disinherited and didn't speak a word to her for seven years.

My dad was hurt too. My older brother was upset with me. Some other people were, also. Our testimony for Christ had suffered.

> We certify the king that, if this city be builded again, and the walls thereof set up, by this means thou shalt have no portion on this side the river.
> Ezra 4:16

Chapter Eight

I WAS STILL INTENT upon making a name for myself. Activities increased after our marriage, much to the consternation of my seventeen-year-old bride. There were all the church meetings. I wanted to be at every one. The softball team I played for took up two nights a week. I was elected an officer in the lodge. My part-time business was increasing. I couldn't understand why Joan did not realize the importance of all these things.

I began to realize things were serious when she left on a trip to Ohio to visit her Aunt Rose, a powerful influence in her life. When she returned from there, things seemed to get worse as I plunged into the affairs of the church and community. Seeing that she needed a change of scenery, we moved to the nearby city of Fort Myers. After ten months of marriage, Joan was found to be with child.

We moved back to Naples into a little rented house on the strip known as "poverty row." America was at war again, this time in Korea. I got my "greeting" in the mail as many other young men in the country did. At the induction center I passed the physical, returned home and awaited my orders. Instead, a notice of exemption arrived in the mail because of Joan's condition.

Two weeks before Christmas, the landlord appeared at our door with an eviction notice. He needed the house. Joan was in her seventh month of pregnancy and we had nowhere to go. We prayed.

Joan's stepmother came to our house in a couple of days and told us that her father had given us a piece of land upon which to build. (He still had not spoken to her.) Over across the bay in East Naples, we walked over the sandy soil. I couldn't believe it. A piece of property all our own. The preacher gave us an old trailer that was suffering from years of use. When it rained on the outside it poured on the inside. But it was home. I hastily built an eight foot square room off to the side of the twenty-four-foot house trailer. That was our home when God gave me a son.

I had fashioned a rough easel out behind the makeshift bedroom and was painting the increasing number of sign jobs that came my way. While outside one night, Joan called for me. She was having some pains.

"Don't worry about it," I said. (I just had to get that job finished!)

A few minutes later she said, "Honey, I think you ought to call the doctor."

I drove down the street to the nearest phone, but he didn't answer. I just had to finish that sign. I tried to reassure her that everything was going to be okay.

"Wally, you better try to call the doctor again!"

Why wouldn't that girl leave me alone for just a few more minutes until I could finish that job? Then I would do anything she wanted me to. At her pleading, I went down the street and tried again. I didn't know. After all, I

EIGHT

had never had a baby. This time he answered the telephone.

"You had better get that girl to the hospital," he said. "I'll meet you there."

The problem was that the nearest hospital was forty miles away in Fort Myers. It didn't seem like I would ever get that sign finished. Our bathing facilities had not materialized yet, so we had to stop enroute at a trailer park up the road from town so Joan could use their facility to take a bath. All the while her labor pains were getting closer together.

Fifteen miles farther north, she made me stop the car so she could get some exercise. After she walked around the car a couple of times, we were on our way again. But she insisted on my stopping for some orange juice before we went to the hospital.

When Joan was finally settled into a room, sedated and properly cared for, I was growing more bone-tired by the minute. I asked how long it would be.

"At least a couple of hours," the nurse said.

Joan was out of it. I decided to go over to town and get a cup of coffee to keep me awake. When I returned to the hospital twenty minutes later, the nurse met me in the hall.

"Where have you been, Mr. Metts? We have been looking all over for you. You are the father of a bouncing baby boy!"

I think I had been unwilling to believe in such a blessing before it came. My nonchalance turned to pure excitement the first time I fully realized that I was a father. There is something indescribable about looking for the first time into the cherub face of a squirming piece of your own flesh and blood. My son has been one of the choice blessings of my multi-blessed life.

DEEP RIVER

We had talked about naming a boy Richard Wing. When Joan came out of her stupor, I shared our good news.

"We have a little boy."

Her next words were the surprise she had been planning for me:

"Wallis Cone Metts, Jr. Wallis Cone Metts, Jr."

She repeated it over and over. What a girl! We nicknamed him "Sailor" because the morning she had started into labor Joan had been out in a boat fishing the canal near our house.

Joan and Sailor came home on Saturday. The preacher came over to our little trailer on Sunday afternoon and spent a precious few minutes with us as, together, we gave our boy back to the God from whom he came. A simple prayer of dedication from the pastor marked the occasion.

But my lovely girl still brooded over the unhappy relationship with her folks. I decided to take her away for a change of scenery. It seemed that in those days we were constantly changing scenery. Back to Augusta we went with our six-month-old son to experience further lessons in the way our Heavenly Father had planned for us. I led the choir in a church there, spoke around the area as a lay preacher, and sold cars in the daytime. Those were hard months. The area was booming when we arrived, but shortly after, the Savannah River Nuclear Plant phased out its construction operation and the economy collapsed overnight. I couldn't give a car away. Half the car lots in town closed up.

It was at that time of leanness that we celebrated our first Christmas with our son. We had been living on blackeyed peas and biscuits and paying eleven dollars a week for our apartment. We didn't have any money for

EIGHT

gifts. I made a small sale at the last minute, and Joan went down to buy a few gifts for Sailor on Christmas Eve while I stayed around the agency to try to sell a car or at least a TV. Christmas Eve morning I had seen a pile of hams in the corner of the showroom for the employees. My mouth fairly watered.

When the day was almost ended, I was called out for a last-minute adjustment on the TV I had sold the day before. When I returned, most of the employees had left. And so had the hams. There was not one in sight. I stood there in the middle of the showroom floor, just before Sailor's first Christmas, with no money and no food, and I cried like a baby. Later, my sympathetic boss found me a ham. And all in all, Christmas was a happy time that year.

By the time we left there, our car had been repossessed, we were dead broke, and God had taught us a valuable lesson. The Lord can give and He can take away. We began to realize that everything was His, and that one of our most pressing needs was to trust Him for our finances.

We arrived back at our little piece of property in Naples with six dollars and no car. I earned seventy dollars the first part of the week we returned, and the Lord got ten percent right off the top. We have been tithing Christians ever since that day. It was January, 1954.

One year later I had to make a financial statement for a business transaction that declared our net worth at $25,000. During that year I had opened my own full-time business, built a guest house on the back of our property, and began to prosper financially. Many of the things I had always wanted began to fall into place. We soon built a larger house, bought a new car, and rapidly ex-

DEEP RIVER

panded the business. We richly enjoyed the blessings that came our way.

But I could not sit and listen to a preacher without wishing that I were there in that pulpit. There was a longing and a surging realization tugging at the reins of my heart. I tried to drown it in activity. I hunted and fished. I actually took my first two-week vacation and traveled north, with Joan and Sailor. We bought waterfront property, intending to build on it someday or sell it at a profit.

Christmas, 1955, was far different from the one two years before. We had lived in the little guest cottage for a couple of years, but now the dream house we had planned since we were kids was completed. We moved in on Christmas Eve. No kid ever had more toys for Christmas than Sailor did that year. We spent hundreds of dollars just on him. I stayed up half the night putting things together, and his childish delight the next morning was worth it all. Of course, two days later he was back in the kitchen playing with the pots and pans.

I had arrived. Everything I had dreamed of had come to pass swiftly. I had a wonderful wife, a healthy son, my own business, money, cars and property. I couldn't understand why it all seemed so empty. Oh, we were not rich by any means. But I was on my way. The potential was there.

But the call to the ministry was as relentless as the earlier call to Christ.

> Speak, and say, Thus saith the
> Lord God; Behold, I am against
> thee, Pharaoh king of Egypt . . .
> which hath said, My river is mine
> own, and I have made it for myself.
> Ezekiel 29:3

Chapter Nine

LOSTMAN'S RIVER, about fifty miles south of Naples, is part of the incredible beauty of the Everglades National Park. A favorite fishing spot for the sports angler and commercial fisherman alike, it empties into Fish Bay and then into the Gulf.

Here, the great white heron watches over a domain of innumerable wildlife. One of the least seen of these species is the pink shrimp. When they are not much bigger than a speck, they start their hundred mile migration from Dry Tortugas to the haven of Florida Bay and its surrounding waters, stretching north through the Ten Thousand Islands. Providing seventy-five percent of the nation's supply of this delicacy, one shrimp may produce 500,000 eggs—a constant supply of food for the redfish, the mangrove snapper and other sought-after prizes of the angler's skill.

The Collier Corporation, largest landowner in Collier County, had decided to dedicate part of its sizeable resources to the opening up of this lush marine frontier to the public. I had become acquainted with a man named

DEEP RIVER

Norman Herron in the Naval Reserve. Someone had told me he worked for the Collier Corporation. As a new man in the outdoor advertising business, I felt any contact would be useful, so I paid him a call one day in Everglades. I dropped my card on his desk and told him I would appreciate it if he could get me some of the company's business.

In a few days calls began coming in from different department heads in the corporation asking me to do various jobs for them. "Mr. Herron told me if I needed anything to call you," they said.

I found out that he was the boss. That was the way our business opened up to growing demands. I hired expert neon and electrical men to provide the technical end of the electrical sign business. A leading artist was brought in from one of the large outdoor advertising companies in Miami. Business was booming. Our outdoor displays soon lined the highways in four counties.

I remember hectic times when a hurricane warning would be out and my whole business would be threatened. We mobilized all our friends and relatives and worked feverishly through many a night to pull down the panels, leaving only the skeletons along the Tamiami Trail to resist the destructive winds. There were happy hours when Joan and I would load a little skiff into the back of a truck and take off to touch up or change the copy on one of our boards. She would sit and watch while I finished a brief chore, and then we would romp together with Sailor in the shallow waters that ran along the Trail.

When ducks were in season, I would load up one of the little boats early in order to be at my duck blind just west of bridge number 66 by daylight. I could get my limit, clean them and be at work by nine in the morning. Nights were often spent camping out in the 'Glades, where I got

NINE

lost more than once.

But it would be unrealistic to say that it was all fun and games. For a young businessman, a rapidly expanding business means plenty of headaches. Much of the money has to be turned back into the business for expansion, and growing pains were almost unbearable at times. The pressure was great, and I had a growing awareness that the pressure was being applied by my Heavenly Father. He had a better plan for me.

One night, Joan came home from an outing to find me trembling on the floor. She thought I had become extremely ill. But I had come to the place where I could not withstand the increasing pressure of God's will for my life. I think she knew without asking. It was one of the hardest decisions I had ever made. My wonderful wife was accustomed to being affluent, and I did not want to deprive her of that kind of life-style. And I feared poverty with a nagging dread. But I had to make a decision or face the consequences of fighting the God who had saved me.

I realized this now, as I looked evenly but tearfully into Joan's face and told her, "I can't run any longer. I've got to answer the call to preach."

We both cried as she suggested we call Rev. E. C. Beaird, our pastor, and discuss the matter with him. When he came over, we sat in the living room of our beautiful home and told him how we felt this new venture was God's will, but we did not see how it could be done. Our obligations were heavy. Members of my family were involved in the business and we did not want to let them down.

Pastor Beaird assured us that, although Satan usually puts many obstacles in the way of doing God's will, if the Lord was leading He would find a way. It was December,

DEEP RIVER

1957, eight years after my conversion.

After reviewing the situation, I first decided to wait for a few months before leaving to begin my training for the ministry. The pastor recommended a school in Chattanooga, Tennessee, and the first of January we drove up to look it over. I set the date for my entry into Tennessee Temple Schools for the following September. But the Lord would not let me put if off.

One night, after the January semester had already begun, I could not sleep. I wrestled with all the alternatives. I had my family to think of. My brother had said he wanted to buy the business and I had to train someone to take my place. There was the matter of renting our house, completing the sale of the business . . . but all my arguments seemed to melt before the insistent demand of the call to preach. I thought that night of how many people I had already failed to reach by waiting as long as I had. A great picture of thousands who might never hear the gospel surged through my mind. I got up in the middle of the night and checked the calendar. Late registration with credit lasted for three more days. I walked into my office the next morning with a startling announcement.

"I'm leaving for college the day after tomorrow," I said to my startled brother.

"Y-you can't! It'll take a miracle to get you out of here in two days," he stammered.

"The Lord's the southeastern distributor on miracles. If it takes one, He will provide it," was my somewhat overzealous answer.

The next two days are a blur. But somehow, we sold the business (making arrangements for monthly payments to help us in school), rented our home and loaded all our belongings in a huge rental trailer with just enough time

NINE

to make the 735-mile trip to Chattanooga before the registrar's office closed Wednesday night, the next day, at 5:30.

The trip was hectic. Somewhere in North Florida, in the middle of the night, I ran out of gas. Locking Joan and Sailor in the car, I started hitchhiking to the next town, wherever that was. The first car that came by came zooming by. He was easily doing a hundred. Way up the road he hit his brakes, screeching to a halt, and put the car in reverse. When the car came to rest beside me, I noticed two suspicious looking characters in the back seat with their collars up around their ears, like you see in gangster movies.

"Get in," the driver growled.

As I opened the door, a pearl-handled revolver lay on the front seat near the spot I was to occupy. I prayed. I glanced quickly back at the car where all my life's treasures were concentrated in one spot, even my wife and son. I didn't know how to refuse the ride that had been offered me. With fear and trembling I got in, and we zoomed off into the night.

Without a word or incident, my strange driver stopped the car in a little town up the road and let me out, while I sent several timely prayers of thanksgiving up to Heaven for a short but safe trip. Local characters were able to tell me where the proprietors of the three local service stations lived, but I could not get any of them to help me. They were absolutely insensitive to the fact that I was stranded with a wife and child on a strange road.

Dejected, I began my walk back to the car. I had seen one other station a couple miles outside of town, and after considerable walking I stopped there. There was a house next door, and I shouted through the front window that I needed help.

DEEP RIVER

"Well, I don't think I can help you," a reply drifted back.

"But I'm stranded down the road here with a wife and a little boy!"

"Who are you?"

"I'm on my way to Chattanooga, Tennessee, to study for the ministry. I have to be there by tomorrow at five-thirty."

"Well, I don't know."

"Please, Mister. I'll pay you anything you want. I need help."

A light shined on me from within the house. A face peered out with a curious caution. I put on my most pleading face.

"What did you say your name was?"

"Metts, Wally Metts. You don't know me. But I sure need help."

He finally came out cautiously, staring intently at me before finally poking around inside the station for a gasoline can. "How much you want?"

"I'll come back and fill up."

"Well, I'll tell you, son. I would have helped you sooner, but they's been some characters coming around places at night with a hard-luck story and robbin' folks. Folks around been mighty careful who they help out."

I breathed an overdue sigh of relief. And I never did find out if the incidents had anything to do with the men who had stopped to give me a ride. With a full tank of gas, we resumed our drive through the night.

In North Georgia the rain began to fall hard. I was trying to be careful with the big trailer, but the hours were rapidly approaching the deadline for my arrival at that business office. We topped a hill, and the trailer began to fishtail going down the steep grade. I wasn't used to driv-

NINE

ing in the hills and I began to panic. I soon lost control of the auto in the two lane highway, forty-one miles from our destination.

"Turn loose of the wheel!" Joan shouted.

I did. When the whole rig came to rest it had made a complete U-turn in the middle of that busy highway without putting a scratch on anything. The 1956 Plymouth station wagon was simply in the wrong lane, headed back toward Florida. Joan, victim of a tragic accident already, was horrified at such things. But when I looked at her, she was smiling.

"Isn't He wonderful?" she asked.

The time deadline came when I reached the city limits of LaFayette, Georgia, some thirty miles south of our destination. I stopped at a public phone booth and dialed the number of Tennessee Temple Schools, asking for the registrar, Mr. David Lockery.

"Mr. Lockery, this is Wally Metts, from Naples, Florida. I don't know if you remember me." I had called him from Naples a couple of days before, informing him of our decision to come earlier than expected.

"How long will you be there?"

"I'm leaving now, Mr. Metts. We have to get ready for prayer meeting tonight."

"Well, I'll never make it in time. But I will go to school without credit this semester, because I am going to start tomorrow."

"Well, I knew you would be here. I have all your things filled out. Just come in five minutes early in the morning and sign a couple of things and you'll be all set."

My college career had begun at the age of twenty-five.

61

> As the valleys are they spread forth, as gardens by the river's side, as the trees of lign aloes which the Lord hath planted, and as cedar trees beside the waters.
> Numbers 24:6

Chapter Ten

FROM THE FOOT of the Great Smoky Mountains, the Tennessee River touches seven states, making its way down across a system of TVA dams as it winds past the Cumberland Plateau, turning north and eventually pouring into the Ohio.

In the eighteenth century, settlers made their way down from the Carolinas into the Tennessee Valley. Early farmers in the valley plied large, creaking boats through its waters using only the current and stern oars as much as a hundred feet long. They moved their produce and supplies by this means, sometimes touching shore at The Suck, a narrow pass between towering Mount Aetna and Signal Mountain. Nearby, clustered around Moccasin Bend, where the river threads the foot of Lookout Mountain, the town of Chattanooga was growing up.

Here, railways making their way south into the states of Georgia and Alabama made this city an important industrial center. A lovely valley city, it lies in a basin surrounded by mountains and hills, mountains with names like Lookout, Signal, Elder, Raccoon and Missionary

TEN

Ridge. It is a part of the Cumberland system, but just a few miles to the east are the Smokies.

The place is rich in history. The last battle of the Revolutionary War was fought here, and one of the most decisive battles of the Civil War, as the determined Yankee foot soldiers scaled the treacherous face of Lookout Mountain and fought the "Battle Above the Clouds," paving the way for Chickamauga and Sherman's march to the sea.

Before the formation of the Tennessee Valley Authority, this area was the scene of numerous and devastating floods. The worst one came in 1867, when it was reported that a steamboat pushed its way down Market Street, the town's main thoroughfare. As in other river towns, settlers stood on the banks in normal times to watch for the approaching steamboats making their way up and down the Tennessee, some of them floating palaces with names like The Shiloh, The Kentucky and The City of Saltillo. Big barges still navigate the Tennessee, passing through the locks of Chickmauga Dam, north of the city.

It was to this lovely city that I came to get an education at Tennessee Temple College. It is a unique institution. Now the second-largest private institution of learning in the state (behind Vanderbilt), it is supported almost entirely by the Highland Park Baptist Church. Dr. Lee Roberson is the imaginative and tireless leader who first put this church, then its schools, on the map. The church presently averages around 10,000 in attendance on Sunday mornings, with more than 5,000 students matriculated in its schools.

The church and schools were only about half that size when I hurried to my first class on a Thursday morning. I thoroughly enjoyed the Christian atmosphere that pervaded the place. Dr. Roberson's forthright stand for the

DEEP RIVER

Bible, separated Christian living and the Second Coming of Christ made a profound effect upon my life. As we studied the Word of God, I gradually developed a bedrock, absolute reliance upon the literal teachings of the Scriptures.

When these convictions form in the heart, there is the awakening of a conscience toward things that are wrong. The great absolutes forming in my heart demanded a philosophy and life-style grounded on the unchanging principles of the Word of God. It is simply not possible to believe these things and not form definite convictions about the world around one. The more the issues of righteousness and morality become clear, the more a forthright stand is called forth. And this kind of stand is usually not welcomed by the world around us, nor is it often understood. When this extreme stance was applied to the problem of alcoholism some years later, I was to meet with unyielding resistance on every hand.

In spite of the wholesome atmosphere of the school, trials awaited us during these years. Joan suffered deeply from the pace. I was taking a full college load, working for an outdoor advertising company, and pastoring a small chapel. We had very little time together. While she was fully in support of my new lifework, she was unsure of her role in it. The new standards were difficult to adjust to, and the pollution of the Chattanooga Valley stirred up a chronic respiratory condition which the Gulf breezes of Naples had prevented.

The financial situation was rough. We had sold our equity in a waterfront lot, made arrangements for a job and arranged a monthly payment through the sale of the business. But a few months after I entered college, my brother suffered bankruptcy. The money we were counting on did not materialize. The job did not work out and

TEN

our savings were soon exhausted.

One night while Joan was in Ohio attending the funeral of an aunt, the whole thing seemed to collapse around me. I had left a business, a home and my family and now found myself in a strange city without any visible means of supporting my family and paying for my education.

I ran out of gas while going downtown in our station wagon, on which we were falling behind in our payments. Clothed only in a Palm Beach suit, I walked along the Chattanooga streets, wondering why I was so cold. Finally, finding a service station, I checked the temperature. It was eight degrees! In Naples, they almost close the schools when it gets down to forty!

At home alone in our tiny three-room flat, cold, scared and dejected, I "had it out" with the Lord. Kneeling beside our bed, I put my finger on Philippians 4:19: "But my God shall supply all your need according to his riches in glory by Christ Jesus."

I emptied my heart. I felt I had taken a step down into poverty again. I was ashamed that I had not adequately provided for a wife and five-year-old son. For the first time in my life I had gone to someone and asked for money to buy groceries. I was totally unprepared for these circumstances. As I recall, I prayed something like this:

> "Lord, this wasn't my idea. You told me You wanted me to do this. You called us away from our home and business. You know how many years I ran from this, Lord. You've got to take care of my wife and boy. I don't know anything else to do but ask You. I have nowhere else to go."

With all my heart I threw my confidence into that verse

of Scripture. The greatest of our prayers are not those which are filled with flowery phrases, but rather those which are called forth out of the extremity of our helplessness and the utter honesty of our hearts.

Somehow, when I rose from my knees that night, I knew God had answered my prayer. And that was where a loving Father had wanted me to be. Up until that time all I knew was to scratch, dig and scheme to accomplish my goals. How merciful God was to teach me to depend on Him!

The next day, three job opportunities opened up. I had to pray about which one to take. We were to see God's hand on our lives in an unusual way for the next few years. He enabled me to finish the four years of college in three and a half years, support my family, pay my college tuition, and pay off some bills I had counted on the income from the business to pay.

The years were hard on Joan, taking a greater toll than I realized at the time. Her health continued to be poor. Chattanooga was extremely polluted in those days, and it resulted in several bouts with bronchial pneumonia. She had already suffered five miscarriages because of a rare blood type, and the pregnancy she experienced in this period was hard and risky. By the time she bore the beautiful blonde daughter I had prayed for, she had almost succumbed to a severe case of bronchial pneumonia. She was confined to the hospital for many days following the arrival of Roselin Toy.

There were some hard lessons I had yet to learn. It did not occur to me how she must have been affected by the long hours of waiting for me to come home from work, then my sitting for long hours reading, or writing a term paper. There were also increasing opportunities for Christian service opening up which I felt obliged to accept. I

TEN

was not to learn for years that every open door does not necessarily have to be entered. Men often do not realize the sacrifices they call upon their wives to endure. Caught up in the excitement of their world-conquering, it is easy to forget the difficulties a wife has waiting in the background while other people consume her husband's time and energy.

Endowed with a sensitive heart, Joan had a tremendous capacity for love. I was not meeting the need. Her positive attitude began to deteriorate, and I reacted by thinking she was unfair in not holding up during a time that required unusual commitment to our goals. But it was not that she wasn't behind me all the way. The problem was that she sensed something in me that I did not see. If I was not sensitive to her needs, and those of the children, how could I be sensitive to the needs of others to whom I must minister in the future? I had not yet discovered that the first priority of a minister of the gospel is to minister to his family.

The things we experienced during this time point up a problem that is too little noticed. Because of my father's alcohol problem, I had not experienced a healthy home environment. Dad's declining power as a man and as a father gave me no adequate father or husband image to learn from. I had no idea how I was failing the wife I had vowed to love. I excused it all because I was involved in a noble work. It is another one of those subtle, innumerable casualties suffered by the alcoholic's family that cannot be measured in dollars.

Other problems arose. When Joan would point out her need, I felt persecuted. Here I was, giving my life for a holy cause, and she didn't understand. How subtle are the traps that lie in wait for us in our spiritual walk! I had determined in my heart to be a different man from the

DEEP RIVER

man I watched my father become. I focused upon making myself different. But Joan, looking at my life, saw that I was the same. When things went roughly for my dad, he went for the bottle. When I experienced rough sailing, I went to work. He was an alcoholic. I was a workaholic. My wife was suffering as my mother had suffered.

Fortunately, her ties to her family in these years grew closer. Aunt Rose, the formidable Ohio woman who had remained unmarried all her life, adopted both of us. Converted in a Billy Sunday meeting in 1911, she caught a vision of what God was trying to do in our lives. The oldest sister of Joan's late mother, Aunt Rose tried hard to fill the vacancy in Joan's life. Many times she would send a check to cover our college tuition or buy groceries. Joan was able to find some refreshing release in frequent trips to Ohio.

On one occasion, her cousin brought his family through Chattanooga on their way to Florida. They attended the little hillbilly chapel where I pastored and got a taste of our "old time religion." When Joan's cousin got back to Ohio, his pastor was preaching a series of messages on the stained glass windows in the sanctuary. The contrast was too much for him. It wasn't long before he relocated his family in a church where the Bible was the focus, and an endearing friendship has resulted with this rugged Ohio farmer, Walt Kaufmann and his family. The deep roots of these Ohio people also met a need in my life, and I happily identified with Joan's kinfolk.

It was while we were in Tennessee that Joan reached an important milestone. In her difficulty to cope with the pace of my college years, she became acquainted with Dr. Philip Marquart, an elderly professor on the staff at Tennessee Temple. Dr. Marquart had been a chief

TEN

psychologist in the European theatre under Eisenhower. A psychiatrist, he had now turned his psychological studies toward the Bible. He was a stabilizing, kindly influence on Joan's life.

In their talks together, he discovered a deep need in her life. Whether her father identified her with her mother, or for some other reason, Joan felt rejected by him. She felt that the other two sisters were more accepted than she, and suffered a terrible feeling of inferiority because of it. Dr. Marquart explained that much of her insecurity came from the fact that she sometimes identified me as a symbol of her father.

"I want him to love me, and I want to love him," she explained about her father. "How can I reach out to him?" she asked.

"The next time you see him, just reach out and touch him. Make physical contact," he said.

We prayed about it. And then the message came that he was going to stop by and see us on his way from Texas to Florida. He had been divorced by Joan's stepmother in Las Vegas, and had moved to Texas, eventually remarrying the woman he had been married to years before, prior to his marriage to Joan's mother. A UPI dispatch carried this interesting item:

> A Florida woman who testified she drove a taxicab while she was pregnant and delivered papers to earn money was granted a divorce and $250,000 Friday from her "nomad" gold prospecting husband.
>
> ... she worked at home in Naples, Fla., during 20 years of marriage while her husband, John, wandered off "like a nomad ... digging for gold in the hills of Nevada and

DEEP RIVER

Arizona" (she said).

District Judge David Zenoff awarded the husband his mining claims, reportedly of little value, and split the $500,000 estate 50-50. Many of the holdings were blue-chip securities and real estate.

When the day came for Dad and Lucy Prince to arrive, we fixed up our little apartment on Missionary Ridge and awaited the event with great anticipation. It was one of those electric moments. He entered with fanfare and spread his massive frame out in one of our little chairs, sphinx-like, in character with the venerable old patriarch who had sired seven children.

For the first time since our marriage Joan and her father talked. The conversation dwelt upon generalities, carefully skirting anything that could arouse a personal response. It dragged on like that until Joan walked over to her dad, put her hands on his shoulders and gently blurted out those life-changing words, "I love you, Dad."

I felt the temperature in the room go up. Years of awkward conversation melted away before those four words, and wounds felt the healing power of the love of God. By the time Dad Prince's baby-blue Cadillac sped out of our driveway, God had done some things in Joan's heart. Much of the insecurity of her life had vanished. They have never had any difficulty communicating since that day.

After being there in Chattanooga about a year, I had accepted the pastorate of the tiny "W" Road Baptist Chapel and was ordained by Highland Park Baptist Church. The small group of worshipers was part of the Highland Park Baptist chapel system, a network of forty-

TEN

five churches located in the Tri-State Area that provided opportunities for students and faculty members to pastor. This chapel was located in a deteriorating old residence with sagging ceilings and rotten floors. An old coal stove provided the heat in winter, and the music was supplied by an ancient pump organ. That is, until my enterprising music director got the idea of hooking up a vacuum cleaner beneath the floor to provide the suction. Then it became an electric organ of sorts.

The poverty of some of the people was unbelievable. It was here that our ministry was fashioned upon the heart-rending necessity of broken lives. Nothing about that ministry was attractive or fashionable. It was hard work, heartbreak and meager results. Were it not for the laughable antics of the hill people and the contagious warmth of the mountain Christians, we might have quit the ministry then and there.

One dear lady could neither read nor write, but she carried the bearing of a mountain queen. Always dressed impeccably, she was a combination of Mary Worth and Dear Abby, with an overflowing supply of the Spirit of Christ thrown in. All she had to do was enter the room and it changed. All those preachers who were to tell me later that women weren't supposed to pray in church had not gotten to me yet. I knew any time I wanted to call upon her to pray, I could bring heaven down into that little chapel!

Since almost nobody lived on "W" Road, that zigzagging highway that hairpinned its way up Signal Mountain, we had to haul most of our crowd from the valley below. Once, I loaded twenty-two people into my Studebaker Lark, with the songleader playing his trumpet all the way down the mountain from his secure position—locked in the trunk.

DEEP RIVER

Even after they paid my salary of fifty dollars a month, we had money left from the congregation, numbering then about fifty, to start a building fund. I started a building program that never got any further than the wooden floor, and eventually rotted away. How many congregations suffer from the overzealous ambitions of young ministers!

My dad came to stay with us awhile during those efforts. The times we spent together working on that chapel were memorable. The neighbors lived up to their "Dogpatch" reputation, standing with folded arms for hours, watching us gather stones, clear ground and build the foundations.

One extremely hot day, one of the girls walked up the hill holding out a tempting pint jar full of ice water for me. It was a welcome gesture, and I was ready for some refreshment. As I turned the bottom of the jar up and guzzled about half of it, Joan, always the practical joker, said, "Wally, there's a worm in that water!"

"Ah, you're crazy," I said as I took another healthy swig.

When I held it out to admire it, sure enough. A big green worm about two inches long was enjoying his swim for the day! This was the same girl who once chased a renegade cat through the chapel at the same time Barbara Drake filled the tiny building with her beautiful soprano voice and a dog howled mournfully from the door outside. Later, I had the sad duty of conducting the funeral of this mentally handicapped girl.

But there were times when the power of God made itself known within the hallowed, weather-beaten walls of that tiny mountain chapel. Men and women were being converted, and I was coming to realize more than ever that there is nothing in the world quite like the life-

TEN

changing gospel of Jesus Christ.

There was also the disappointment of seeing that some people would never be reached. Down behind the chapel, one of our women had moved into a small, unfinished home with her alcoholic husband. Since they were so close, we witnessed to him, wept for him and prayed for his deliverance, all to no avail. Little did I know that the little mountain home I visited so often would, years later, play such an important part in our lives.

Graduation day came in August, 1961. A college education is not a very big deal these days, but it was a moment of satisfaction for me. I could not remember any male member of the Metts clan who had ever done it. At the age of 29, I did not consider going on to seminary.

The completion of our studies in Chattanooga and departure came about with a typical hillbilly flair. During all our time in college, our plans were to return to Naples, move back into our beautiful home and begin scheduling evangelistic meetings. The Lord had already opened up a number of meetings and my dream of becoming an itinerant evangelist seemed to have arrived. Our former Naples pastor, Calvin Beaird, had solved our moving problems. His wife had inherited a 1929 Chevrolet ton-and-a-half truck. It was in mint condition, having spent most of its life in a garage in LaFayette, Georgia.

We loaded all our earthly belongings on the flat bed of this imposing old antique, which we affectionately named "The Lump." At the last minute, my boss prevailed upon me to remain in Chattanooga for a week to help him finish up some jobs. Joan's sister and brother-in-law had come to my graduation and they took turns driving "The Lump" 735 miles to Naples.

The mechanical brakes on this thirty-two-year-old monstrosity almost burned up before they got to the bot-

DEEP RIVER

tom of Missionary Ridge. Joan told me tales of the romance of wheeling that tireless old vehicle into service stations, while sightseers gathered to peer into its ancient cab and listen to the "uh-ooga" of its bulb horn. My lovely, laughable bride moved home in style, looking for all the world like one of the Beverly Hillbillies!

Graduation had been on Monday. Friday, while I finished up the last few chores I would ever do for Faulkner Outdoor Advertising, a long distance call came from Joan. A church in Fort Myers, Florida, was without a pastor and wondered if I could fill in for them on Sunday. And so my college days ended as they had begun—in a rush!

I pointed my little Lark toward South Florida, driving all night Friday and most of the day Saturday to keep my speaking engagement only one week after Dr. Roberson had placed that piece of sheepskin in my hand.

> She sent out her boughs unto the sea, and her branches unto the river.
> Psalm 80:11

Chapter Eleven

THE CALOOSAHATCHEE is a mile wide where it passes the downtown section of Fort Myers, Florida. Its waters are brackish a little way inland, but grow more salty as they flow toward Pine Island, Sanibel and the Gulf. Towering palms greet the visitor who approaches the city from the north. In the waters near the south shore, a beautiful yacht basin lends the beauty of boats to its enchanting appeal.

A young inventor named Thomas Alva Edison discovered this place when it was young and primitive. He had come here in search of a filament to perfect the light bulb. He had the idea that the answer might lie in the bamboo plants that grew plentifully along the Caloosahatchee. The bamboo idea didn't work out that well, but Edison stayed to set up his winter home and laboratory here.

Local lore says when Edison had finally perfected the light bulb, he offered to furnish enough bulbs free to light up the downtown streets. All the city council had to do was furnish the poles. But there was a complication. A

DEEP RIVER

pond in the middle of town attracted the cows, who came up to drink and spend the night. They say the official minutes of the city council state the reason for turning down Edison's offer: "It would keep the cows awake!"

Edison was once even denied entrance to the plush Naples Hotel, 40 miles south in Naples, because of his shabby appearance. By the time an astonished manager had related his apology, Edison had decided he didn't care to eat in the hotel's uppity dining room.

It was in Fort Myers that I began my full-time ministry, pastoring a small Baptist church until they could obtain a pastor. Or so I thought.

Momentous events were making themselves felt in those days. Martin Luther King had awakened the blacks to a new political fervor. In Chattanooga we had seen the fire department hose down a crowd of blacks attempting to stage a downtown lunch counter sit-in. While many southern-bred whites like myself had to admit to an unsettling color line, there were greater fears. We were fearing what the consequences would be when the long arm of Washington began to reach into local schools and governments. It was not only a confrontation between races, but between states' rights and civil rights. Just how much could the government guarantee the rights of all individuals without hampering the rights of all?

Alan Sheppard had just launched America into the space age, and national and world philosophy took on a mind-expanding jolt. For science, the sky was no longer the limit, and secular humanism pushed the god, Knowledge, higher upon its pedestal of adoration. We were now entering the age of the full-fledged philosopher-scientist, experimenting with such uncanny ideas as the creation of man in a test tube and genetic engineering.

America was deepening its involvement in a divisive

ELEVEN

war in Indochina, an issue which threatened to wrench governmental authority from its roots. Young people, disenchanted with the materialistic values of their parents, had spawned the hippie culture with its world of drugs, anarchy and free sex. Thinking the war in Vietnam to be meaningless in their value system, they burned draft cards and flags in mass demonstration against establishment America.

Violence had become commonplace. The Kennedy brothers, Martin Luther King and even the alleged assassin, Lee Harvey Oswald, fell to the assassin's bullet. A spiraling crime rate had made America's cities unsafe and turned ghettos into battlefields. The public school system was hastening the decline that made itself known in drugs, vandalism and student revolt. Rock and protest music had become the medium of expression that preached a gospel of degeneracy to a new, "turned-on" generation.

A man cannot minister in a vacuum. His message must be preached in the context of the times. Although the pure gospel is unchanged by the wildest antics of men, our frame of reference cannot help but be shaped by the events of our world. And these tumultuous times forged the anvil upon which men of influence would shape their convictions after the "sick sixties."

Approximately eighty-five people gathered in the modest auditorium of the church Sunday morning when Joan, Sailor, and Toy accompanied me to that first service. The Lord was pleased to bless our message and grant fruit that morning. That night, the crowd was about as large. I preached from II Chronicles 7:14 about the need for revival. The Lord had prepared the hearts of the people, and the great majority of them responded to the message with conviction.

DEEP RIVER

Although I had not known it, the chairman of the deacons had been brutally murdered three months before I arrived. The people, stunned by the tragedy, had been praying for God to do something in their lives and their church. That morning, the church experienced the beginning of a spiritual revival that was to last for three years, wonderfully touching hearts.

It became evident after a few services that we were going to have to consider whether to accept a call to the pastorate of that church. We felt led of the Lord to accept, and I had to move Joan and the children out of our home a month after we had moved in.

Joan had another testing the last night she stayed there. We had hauled the furniture to the small pastorium of the church, leaving her in Naples to spend one last night.

She walked into the empty living room and spread her blanket out on the wood floor that she had polished to a gleaming luster. Lying down on the floor, she stared up at the stained beams of the cathedral ceiling and began to cry. Her sister walked in from next door, lay down beside her and cried too. Joan had just come through a long, hard struggle in Tennessee. Another one now lay ahead.

Finally, alone with her thoughts, she took her case to the God of all comfort. After a time of prayer and honest searching, she seemed to hear God speaking to her about that house. "How would you like to live in this house in Heaven?" She realized that if sacrifices were easy, they would not be sacrifices.

It wasn't easy, but this young woman, reared in a Gold Coast home, had to put that house on the altar of sacrifice that night. It is one thing for a man to give his life. It is even more difficult to ask it of his wife. But God does not require sacrifice without giving something more precious in its place, and not only more sacrifices but

ELEVEN

many more blessings were in our path.

A little while after we began this pastorate, Dad began to visit more frequently. One Sunday night, I was preaching on the love of God. I could tell he was responding to what I said. I wanted him to know that not only I, but God loved him as well.

"The Bible does not attempt to define the love of God," I said, "but the depth of His love is sounded in the words, 'For God so loved . . .' He so loved that He did not quit giving until He exhausted Heaven's riches, giving His only begotten Son, Heaven's most glorious and best. The poet, unable to find words to describe this love, could only say,

> Could we with ink the ocean fill,
> And were the skies with parchment made;
> Were every stalk on earth a quill,
> And every man a scribe by trade;
> To write the love of God above
> Would drain the ocean dry.
> Nor could the scroll contain the whole
> Though stretched from sky to sky.

"There is no limit to the love of God. He can reach from the highest heights to the lowest depths, and He can reach you tonight!"

On the first verse of the closing song, Dad came to the front of that little auditorium, threw his arms around my neck, and told me he wanted the Saviour about whom I had preached. I was so overcome I had to ask a deacon to close the service—while I rushed back to my study. There, years of hurt were washed away in the sobs of my joy and relief.

Until his death, I held to the conviction that Dad had

DEEP RIVER

experienced a true conversion, although he never enjoyed complete deliverance from alcohol. There were long periods of abstinence after that, along with a marked increase in interest in spiritual things. There was a closeness we enjoyed in the following years we had not known before.

But most people do not understand the symptoms of the last stages of alcoholism. I have had many people tell me, "The gospel is the only answer to the alcohol problem." That is true. By the time Dad had made his decision, he had reached the stage of the "street people," those pathetic derelicts who sleep in the alleys and skid rows of the world. Armies of dedicated Christian workers minister in the rescue missions and other ministries which have a special burden for this very needy kind of person. It takes a special kind of grace. By some estimates, less than two percent of those who make decisions for Christ after they have reached this stage ever recover completely enough to return to normal life.

Alcohol is a toxic drug. Slowly, systematically it eats away the tissues of every organ in the body, the brain and nervous system. The respiratory and circulatory tissues deteriorate rapidly in the final stages. Even the slightest consumption of ethyl alcohol produces dead cells in the brain, the only tissue in the body that does not replace itself. When a man has been drinking steadily for years, this lethal poison takes its toll on the brain. By the time Dad made his decision for Christ, his manhood had wasted away and he had lost his ability to think clearly. His physical resources had been depleted to the point at which the damage was irreversible.

When a man gets in a fight and has his eye put out, God does not restore his eye after conversion. And the pathetic damage done to the body of an alcoholic usually

ELEVEN

stays with him even after his soul is restored.

Almost every program dealing with alcoholism is geared toward treating the victim after he has succumbed to its horror. Despite all the scientific studies on the subject, one disturbing fact remains: nobody has ever become an alcoholic without alcohol. It is not caused by a certain combination of physical and mental characteristics in the unfortunate individual. It is caused by alcohol, pure and simple. And until our generation can face that fact, alcohol will continue to produce the greatest social problem in the United States.

Ostensibly, prohibition was repealed because of the violence linked to the illegal trade. I have records from the U.S. Treasury Department showing that the last year prohibition was in effect, ten treasury agents and a few policemen were killed. Some mobsters were also gunned down. But, *every year, alcohol kills 200,000 Americans, costs the nation 25 billion dollars in lost production and other expense and adds to the current crop of 10 million alcoholics in this country.* One wonders if it is worth the price.

Actually, these official HEW figures for the year 1975 are conservative. A subsequent report by Dr. Stuart Schweitzer of the University of California at Los Angeles reports the alcohol loss at:

> lost production, $20.6 billion
> health, $11.9 billion
> vehicle accidents, $6.6 billion
> fire protection, highway safety and the
>   criminal justice system, $2.7 billion
> violent crimes, $2 billion
> fire losses, $375 million

which makes a staggering total loss, due to alcohol, of

DEEP RIVER

$44.17 billion! That the whole industry is a total loss is seen by the fact that total tax revenues in 1975 were only $8 billion, and the industry only grossed $27 billion.

The years at that Baptist church in Fort Myers were filled with blessing and trials, but God was teaching us many lessons. For three years, very few Sundays went by without somebody giving his life to Jesus Christ. We built a 500 seat auditorium and began a bus ministry. The men's cottage prayer meetings, started before I came, continued throughout with many answers to prayer. The church purchased a new home for us to live in, and this first pastorate seemed a considerable success. It went from nineteenth in size in its association to fourth, judged by average attendance.

But the convictions formed in my heart during college years were leading me to take more of a separatist stand. After much thought and prayer, I knew I must leave that particular association. The beloved congregation was shocked when I read my resignation one Sunday morning, sadly relating the reasons why I felt it necessary to follow my personal convictions. Some ugly things were said about us, and much misunderstanding accompanied my move. But I can honestly say that these people loved me, and I loved them. Brothers in Christ, we will sort it all out someday as we rejoice together on the banks of the River of Life.

One blessing of that three and a half years of ministry was the arrival of our third and last offspring, a black-eyed, dark-skinned beauty named Julian Joy. We began to affectionately call our brood Joy, Toy and "Boy." These wonderful children were going to provide some sorely needed balm as we went into the next three and a half years, a period in our life we call "the great tribulation."

> Turn again our captivity, O Lord,
> as the streams in the south.
> Psalm 126:4

Chapter Twelve

HENDERSON CREEK runs along Shell Island Road down to Shell Island and the Gulf of Mexico. Barefoot Williams, that mysterious recluse who raised a "barrel of kids," had his place hid away a few miles off the Tamiami Trail where this creek winds along past mangroves, marshes and occasional little beaches on which the fiddlers played, and gators and turtles came out to sun. Folks said that when somebody in his family died, he would just go out and bury them in his backyard, but I never asked him if it was true, so I don't know.

A little south of here by water, Goodland Point, Caxambas and Marco Island formed a fisherman's paradise. That was before the developers heard about it, building one of those instant cities that had become so common in the state. In the waters that stretched from here to Shark River, commercial fishermen would occasionally get rich after dark, hauling huge loads of prey from the rich waters of the Ten Thousand Islands.

The Prince farm, 150 acres of palm-studded tropical dirt, bordered on Shell Island Road. When Mr. Prince

DEEP RIVER

visited us in Chattanooga, he said he planned to give us that property to use as a conference grounds. How we loved that place! We fixed up the old ramshackle farmhouse with its rusty tin roof, mowed acres of ground and began to use the place as a private retreat, dreaming of the day when we could have the money to develop it into a youth camp and haven for retired missionaries. It was typical of this period of our lives. We were pioneering.

The Southwest Florida area did not understand the kind of religion I was preaching in those days. With the exception of two tiny, primitive missions, all the Baptist churches in the whole area were in the domain of the association we had just left. And while I did not fight other groups, my preaching had taken on the tone of the Fundamentalist, sternly entrenched in the literal interpretation of the Scriptures. Most people unacquainted with the theological issues still do not understand what a Fundamentalist is. The picture most people see is an ignorant, backwoods character who is not much removed from the seventeenth century. Actually, the Fundamentalist would like to think his doctrine is closer to the first century. A Fundamentalist is simply a person who tries all issues and creeds by the fundamental teachings of the Scriptures.

During the eight years we spent in the area, I was able to help in the starting of a number of churches that flourished under a more autonomous, strictly Biblical banner. The first one began after Ivan Burley had joined our first Fort Myers church. He was tongue-tied from birth, and it took me awhile to even know what he was telling me. Shortly after that, he was transferred to Marco Island to work in the Rod and Gun Club there. When I got a letter from Ivan complaining that there was no church on the island to attend, I told him we would just start one. We met and talked it over.

TWELVE

"Ivan, I'll set up a meeting in a home on Marco Island, and you tell everyone to come if they are interested in starting a Baptist church."

"Okay, I'll do dat," he said.

I think Ivan knocked on every door on that island. I can imagine what the residents—rough weather-beaten old fishermen and northern retirees—thought when this man came to their door and in halting, almost unintelligible speech, told them we wanted to start a church on Marco Island.

When the appointed time came, we met with a few folks in a home and announced a revival meeting in the old clapboard community meeting house. Dale Vessell, an ordained minister who was teaching in the public schools, agreed to be the pastor. The people packed out that little meeting house as I preached night after night. We took a handful of transplanted Baptists and the converts from that meeting and organized the First Baptist Church of Marco Island.

That simple process was repeated several times during these pioneering years as a network of Independent Baptist Churches began to spring up in the Southwest Florida area. Other preachers moved in and started churches also. Today there are a number of Independent Baptist churches in every major community of the Southwest Florida area.

We started the Fort Myers Baptist Church in the center of town, renting a tiny church building from the Christian Science people. In a few weeks, our attendance had reached a hundred and we began to look for property that afforded more room for parking and expansion.

In order to support my family, I went to work for a sign painter, then became a superintendent of construction in a large development on Cape Coral. Some people may frown on that, but I figured if the Apostle Paul could make tents, I could work to support my ministry. When the work became large enough to support us, we again accepted a financial sacrifice and went full-time for the church. Somehow, that caused trouble and looking back I guess I am guilty of not properly training the people to take care of a pastor.

An unbelievable series of circumstances began to unfold in our lives. After leaving a good-paying job and accepting a less than adequate salary, I began to get disturbing news from two banks in the city. I had foolishly co-signed notes for a couple of people in trouble, and both of them had defaulted! Then a collection agency began to call us every day to collect a bill we had no record of, which we finally learned belonged to a relative.

In the midst of all this, I came home from church one day after Joan had been to the doctor. She was out in the backyard of our lovely old Spanish-style home, hanging clothes on the line. I walked up to her with no preparation for what she was about to say.

"What did the doctor say, Honey?"

I'll never forget that look. The faint hint of a teardrop glistened on her cheek as she turned, looking wistfully into my eyes.

"He said I have cancer," she said.

You don't exactly hear that from your wife every day in the week. The color drained from my face, and I did not know what to say. Silently, we walked into the house after we finished hanging the clothes. I held her in my arms and told her how much I loved her. We prayed together and asked God to intervene. Silently, I began to search my heart, trying to find out all the areas in my life that were failing God. It did not add to my strength to find that there were many.

TWELVE

The next day, while I was away, the man from the collection agency called again and Joan went to pieces. When I got home and learned of it, I flew into a rage. I dialed his number.

"Did you call my wife today?"

"Yes, Mr. Metts, I called her again about that past due account."

"Did I or did I not tell you we didn't owe you that money?"

"I can only go by our records, Mr. Metts."

"Were you aware of my wife's condition?"

"I'm only trying to do my job, Mr. Metts."

I was not thinking rationally. "I'll tell you what I'll do, Mister. You call my house and bug my wife one more time, and I'll personally come down to that office and break every bone in your body!" I shouted into the phone.

"W-W-Why, Mr. Metts. You're supposed to be a Reverend!"

"And, Mister, you're supposed to be a gentleman," I said just before I pushed the receiver halfway through the base of the telephone.

That's miles away from the way a minister is supposed to talk to anybody. But I felt I was being pushed to the breaking point. By now the church owed me a thousand dollars in back salary, and I had made it a policy in my ministry never to make money an issue. It was hard to keep biting my lip, because the men of the church had come to me and asked me to leave the profitable job I had, and I gladly did it to be more effective in my ministry. I couldn't understand why people could not be more sensitive to the needs of a pastor and his family.

But this was just the beginning. And the more pressure increased, the more I felt crushed. All the awful, inferior feelings returned. I simply could not accept the fact that all this was not because of some awful sin. I wrestled daily with everything in my life, trying desperately to make myself perfect so God could bless me. The truth was, the more I looked at myself, the more I became spiritually weaker. I had seen Dad agonize that way many times over his drinking.

I have found that very often alcoholics are people who expect perfection of themselves, proud people who think they are capable of the utmost in performance. When they fall far short of that ideal, they entertain a kind of emotional suicide, ever drowning in the agony of defeat. How badly I needed to understand and appreciate the grace of God! It was not that Dad was to blame for the way I felt, but I could see myself succumbing to the same weaknesses he did. As I identified with him I wanted to hide from the defeat and pain.

It is strange that in the midst of such weaknesses God can continue to bless. While we were having problems with personalities in the church, the gospel was still powerful and effective. People were coming to Christ. We had purchased seven and a half acres of land on the outskirts of town.

Renting the community center in nearby Charlotte Harbor, we preached for two weeks before we turned a nucleus of people over to the compassionate and able man who had a vision for a work there, Ray Thompson. The Charlotte Independent Baptist Church is a powerful witness in that community today.

We had engaged a fine young assistant pastor who was a great help to us, and calls continued to come in for me to preach in meetings all over the United States. Nobody knew I was dying on the inside.

> Then I proclaimed a fast there, at the river of Ahava, that we might afflict ourselves before our God, to seek of him a right way for us, and for our little ones, and for all our substance.
>
> Ezra 8:21

Chapter Thirteen

WHISKEY CREEK bisects McGregor Boulevard, a picturesque road lined on both sides with stately Cuban Royal Palms, a uniquely beautiful thoroughfare. A visiting man from South Carolina once told me he thought these straight, gray trees were made of concrete. He could not resist the temptation one day to stick his pocket knife in one when nobody was looking to see if it was really a trunk of wood.

It was on a shore of the Caloosahatchee, not far from Whiskey Creek, where Joan and I were to win one of those victories necessary in the life of Christian, the struggling, alien pilgrim who makes his way toward a better land.

While we were waiting for Joan to have the surgery the doctor had prescribed, we got away for a day for a conference in Tampa. Raymond Hancock, pastor of Providence Baptist Church in a Tampa suburb, was hosting the conference. He was also a pilot, and he frequently flew in and out of a small airstrip behind the church for both work and pleasure. During a break in the conference, a

DEEP RIVER

friend and I heard the revving of an engine and a loud thud. At the time I thought it was a truck working somewhere back in the fields that lay beyond the woods.

As we returned to the dormitory, a man rushed up white-faced. "Ray just cracked up his plane!"

Ray's assistant pastor arrived on the scene as the news came, and the two of us jumped into his car to make the twenty minute ride to the hospital where he had been taken. Arriving at the back entrance to the emergency room, we walked briskly up the corridor to where I saw a startling sight. There, on a stretcher in the corridor, lay my six-year-old daughter, Toy! Until that moment, I had not known she was a passenger in that plane. I went into temporary shock until the truth penetrated my unbelieving mind.

We were to find that Ray Hancock, one of his men and two young girls had gone up for a short spin around the area between services. The Piper aircraft had failed from fuel starvation, and Ray had managed to miss the trees surrounding the airfield, nosing the craft down in the middle of a pasture. It came to rest with the tail pointing straight up, shoving the four people mercilessly into the forward cowl of the plane. It was a miracle any of them survived. Toy suffered a concussion and had to remain in the hospital for several days, but was not otherwise affected.

Joan's surgery was considered successful, removing all sign of cancer tissue. We gave God great thanks for that. Meanwhile, I had to begin moonlighting to pay the rising bills. That only complicated the troubles I was having with some of the folks in the church. The series of events were incredible. One deacon was harassing me each time I preached from the Old Testament, saying I was taking the church back under the law. Another claimed he had seen

THIRTEEN

me romancing one of the young women in the church. One man boldly proclaimed that black people had no souls, so we ought to drop our support for African missionaries and forbid blacks to attend our church. Another board member wanted me to sign a statement that I would not sue the church for the back salary they owed me. I had never even mentioned it.

I am sure that under different circumstances, such things would never have happened. But feelings were running strong. Satan was having a field day. To make matters worse, I was reeling from the incredible events of my life. I was on the defensive, and I am sure that my messages did not reflect the victorious, assured confidence that is necessary to lead a flock to spiritual success.

Suddenly, without warning, my assistant's wife left him. That only added fuel to the fire. There seemed to be no limit to the rushing flood of trouble. People had long since sensed something wrong, and were leaving the church. I felt I had lost my ability to minister to that congregation. Wearily, one Sunday morning two and a half years after I began that work, I read my resignation to the congregation.

Joan and I got in our car and drove down to the riverside one day. Under the coconut palms on a grassy place, we held our arms around one another and wept. We could not fit the things that were happening into any kind of sensible pattern. There was no doubt in our minds that God had called us, or that He was fitting all this into some kind of plan. When a person is under the surgeon's knife, it is hard to understand the art of the surgeon. You only know you're hurting. In the hurt and confusion, we could only vow our love to one another once again and decide to stay in there. Whatever the course of this river

DEEP RIVER

we were caught up in, we were sure God knew the end of it.

For the first time in my ministry, I became a "candidate" for a church. At Marcus Hook, near Philadelphia, Pennsylvania, I preached in a church with an attendance of around 500, two new buses paid for that were not being used and $60,000 in a building fund for a new building. The Sunday morning service was broadcast live to the city of Philadelphia. We were not in any hurry to make a decision.

A church in Tampa with fine potential contacted me and I preached for them in both services, informing them that I could not make a decision for a month. The Sunday evening service, in particular, was especially fruitful. To my consternation, they voted unanimously to call me the following Wednesday night. I told them I could not give them an answer right away.

A church in St. Petersburg, with a beautiful pastorium which Joan really liked, asked me to come and speak. The Lord seemed to bless and the people were warm and interested. We were waiting on the Lord.

Meanwhile, some of the folks at our church in Fort Myers kept asking us to reconsider and stay. I explained that I thought my relationship to the board members would not permit it. Since we were still serving out our notice, a member of the church stood up one Wednesday night and made a motion we dissolve the board of deacons! Someone seconded it, and before I knew it, Southside Baptist Church (we had changed the name) was without deacons. Prayerfully, we considered staying. It is not easy to leave a work that your heart and soul have gone into.

Reluctantly, I made the decision to stay with the church that had by now dwindled to a small number. I wrote to

THIRTEEN

the three churches we were considering and informed them of my decision.

Hindsight is much better. It is hard to discern the leadership of God at times. Looking back in retrospect, I now wonder if I was even wise in leaving that first Baptist church which I pastored fresh out of college. I know if God had been in it, He could have worked out the difference in doctrine in time. I wonder if I should ever have stayed at Southside. The following year was not to see any great improvement.

But whatever mistakes in judgment we might make, one thing is for sure. God is still able to turn our defeats into His victories. If I spent three and a half years out of the will of God, He at least was able to use the hardships of that period to form character in our lives and teach us some of the richest lessons we ever learned. And little did I realize that the lessons learned with such difficulty would some day crystalize into my first published book, *The Brighter Side*.

The next year brought some pleasant experiences as well. We went on a preaching mission to the West Indies, where I preached every night in the Island Harbor Baptist Church in Anguilla for missionary Freeman Goodge. Joan sang each night, and although that little island was locked in a struggle for independence from Britain, it was a high experience for us.

The sales job I had taken earned us a trip to Nassau, where we cruised aboard a luxury liner and shopped the quaint shops. God has a way of dropping "handfuls on purpose" even in the hardest of times. His river of grace contains just the right combination of adventure and refreshment to make the Christian life exciting.

But there were more bumps on the way. It was a disappointment to us when the farm land became too valuable to give away, and was sold to developers. Dad had been living there, and his condition seemed to be getting progressively worse. Preachers have to grapple with the problem of the sovereignty of God. If it all depends upon the way man behaves, then all is lost, for man has always failed.

I guess I had knocked on a thousand doors to proclaim the gospel of Jesus Christ. I could not count many out of that vast number who really followed through to live successful Christian lives. And yet, I knew how my own life had been dramatically changed by the gospel in one instant in a Sunday evening service. And I had seen others literally transformed. If God is sovereign, and He is in charge, then all of man's failure, unbelief and weakness does not change the Person of God. He remains the same.

But for now, I seemed to be going nowhere. I had left my business to enter the ministry. In all honesty, I would have to say my second full-time pastorate had been a failure, as my personal standards went. I was now thirty-six years old. My future was very uncertain, and I longed for one of those nice, settled pastorates I had turned down. I drove our old, beat up jeep out across the Caloosahatchee to North Fort Myers and pulled into a secluded palmetto clump. I sat with my back against a pine tree, opened my New Testament and began to read the Gospel According to Matthew.

I don't know how long I was there, praying and searching. Everybody occasionally thinks God has forgotten they are there. I reminded Him of how much I had "given up" to follow Him and how badly things had gone for us. I was really feeling sorry for myself. How quickly we forget the blessings and focus on the testings! After a long while, I looked up to see a tiny little bird flitting across the palmetto branches, not three feet away. He

THIRTEEN

paused, cocked his head, and looked curiously my way.

I started talking to him. (I'm glad nobody was around.)

"Little bird, here you are in this big world, hidden in the palmettos. Just think, nobody knows you are here except me. Well, not exactly. God knows you're here."

I was reminded that not even a sparrow can fall to the ground that He does not see. He had not forgotten me at all. He who counted both the stars and the sparrows, also had numbered the very hairs of my head. And every strand of the weaving of my life was a part of His workmanship.

> And the likeness of their faces
> was the same faces which I saw by
> the river . . .
> Ezekiel 10:22

Chapter Fourteen

IN THE TEXT ABOVE, Ezekiel was talking about his vision of the cherubs, like those which circle around the throne of God. At the River Chebar, he had seen these living creatures, who have a special purpose in God's kingdom. And the writer of the Book of Hebrews says by entertaining strangers, many of us have entertained angels unaware.

I am reminded of the first time I looked into the cherubic faces of each of our three children. And they have been special emissaries from God. The grace of God can use children to fill their parents' lives with sunshine and happiness. Our kids have lightened our way through all our lives. As parents, we are unspeakably thankful for the companionship and joy of those three wonderful cherubs.

Our son has almost never caused us disappointment. Since others have shared that evaluation, we do not feel that it is merely the blind judgment of doting parents.

It is not that we have been such good parents. We have known parents who showed much more promise than we,

FOURTEEN

but have seen great heartbreak come through the lives of their children. It is hard to explain why God, in His grace, sometimes spares some parents the hurt that others have to endure. Not only a bright and compassionate son, but two wonderful daughters have been given to us.

Toy is a born skid talker, like her mother. She thinks one thing, but another sometimes comes out. We can never forget the time she looked out a car window at the heavy mists that drifted across the fields and said, "The frog is out today." Or the time she read a "cash and carry" sign in front of a store and called it, "catch and hurry!" Practical, level-headed and industrious, she has lent a rare quality to our family life.

I had always dreamed of a little blonde girl, running through the house and filling it with sunshine. She has never given us any reason to doubt her love or question her submission to our authority. Our children have been reared by tough standards. Forbidden to go to certain places and required to abstain from certain practices, they have practiced obedience without rebellion until this day. It is a serious mistake for parents to believe authoritarian upbringing will result in eventual rebellion. Most kids are honest enough to want to know where they stand. Of course, we have built our family in the unfeigned love of God. Unashamedly, we have expressed our love to one another often, lest any of us should forget.

During our period of testing in Fort Myers, little Joy was especially a joy. Once, while we went to Tampa to retrieve Toy from the hospital after the plane crash, we left a church bus parked behind our house. We did not realize that a city ordinance prohibited the overnight parking of anything larger than a pickup truck in that residential neighborhood.

DEEP RIVER

One of our neighbors turned us in. Wally, Jr. (Sailor) and little five-year-old Joy were home alone when a big burly policeman walked up to our front door and knocked. Joy answered the door.

"Hi, is your daddy home?"

"Uh-uh."

"How about your mommy?"

"Nope."

"Are you here by yourself?"

"Nope."

"Well, who's here besides you?"

"My brother, Sailor."

"Would you call him, please?"

She placed her hands on her hips, walked to the center of the living room and hollered, "Sailor! The cops are here!"

Once while we were just sitting down for the evening meal, this five-year-old sprite announced with triumph, "Every night after everybody has gone to bed, Tina (the little girl next door) and I go out and chase booglars!"

None of us had the slightest idea what a booglar was. It sounded like a cross between a burglar and a bogey man. Straining to keep a straight face, I asked, "Where do you chase them?"

"We chase them through the sky. Last night, I tore the moon half in two chasing a booglar through the sky."

"I see. What do you do with them when you catch them?"

"We kill them. It's not nice to kill people, but it's all right to kill booglars."

"You—uh—kill them, huh? How?"

"I killed them last night with a butcher knife."

"How do you get out of the house when it's all shut up?" her brother asked.

FOURTEEN

"See that little hole in the screen? I push my belly button and it makes me real little. Then I can get out through the hole!"

It was too much. We simply could not continue the conversation in that vein. Children live in a wonderful world of imagination. And they are so frank! Once, years before, I had questioned Toy when she was that age to see if she could tell someone how to find her way home if she were lost. After helping her to memorize our street number and phone number, I drilled her on them, questioning her until she could give the correct answer. I thought to carry the matter a little further.

"What is your daddy's name, little girl?" I asked as if I were a stranger.

"Revun Wally Metts."

"Where does he work?"

"The Bap'ist Chu'ch."

"What does he do there?"

"He takes care of de babies an' sweeps de floors."

I think they have gained a strong sense of security from the down-to-earth, practical values of their mother. She has seldom been afraid of anything God ever made. There was one never-to-be-forgotten night when I may have saved the life of a prowler. We had knelt together to have prayer, when I became aware of her absence from the side of the bed. I spoke her name softly, but she didn't answer. Stepping into the hall, I flipped on the light and called her name aloud.

"Shhhh! Turn off that light!" she scolded.

Before I could ask what was happening, she blurted out, "Oh, you scared him away!"

She explained to me that she had walked into the darkened kitchen and spotted a prowler outside in our yard. He would walk hurriedly from one tree to the other.

DEEP RIVER

By the time I turned on the hall light, she was standing on the screen porch, gun in hand, watching every move he made!

"Children are an heritage of the Lord." One of the most unfortunate philosophies abroad today is that children are a heritage of the state. When Wally was in the tenth grade (at the age of 14) permission was requested for him to read Salinger's *Catcher In The Rye*. I had not heard of it, so I requested that a copy of it be sent home.

I was utterly shocked at the few pages I read. I had been exposed to such gutter language before my conversion, but I was appalled that it was being assigned to a fourteen-year-old boy in a school classroom. The teacher's explanation was that he would be exposed to it sometime, and it would be better to be there! I said that it would be over my dead body!

My contention was that God had given me those children, and my responsibility to rear them in His way did not end because I dropped them off at some schoolhouse. I felt I was still responsible to God for what they learned. And the things I saw in the public schools were giving me no little concern. It is strange that so many parents have delegated the responsibility for teaching their children to teachers they do not know, philosophies with which they do not agree, and textbooks they have never read.

About this time, I had pulled my car over to a picnic area on the Bonita Causeway and again had a time of searching the will of God for my life. A wonderful peace had come into our lives now, and I was ready to launch out in faith into the field of evangelism. Meetings had begun to open. In Bible conferences I was sharing a new series of messages learned in the crucible of testing, called

FOURTEEN

"The Blessings of Affliction." I had discovered in the Bible that there were certain blessings that could only come through the medium of testing and trial.

And I sensed a new power in my preaching. In Lake City, Florida, numbers of people trusted Christ in a revival meeting. In Louisville, Kentucky, a pastor who called me for a meeting had only 65 in his Sunday School the first Sunday. In that meeting, 55 people gave their lives to the Lord. The church did not have a baptistry, and no converts had been baptized. He mixed the mortar for me while I laid up a concrete block baptistry out in the middle of the floor, where the future location of the pulpit was to be. We filled it up with water from a garden hose, and that Sunday he baptized 28 people!

In small country churches and big city churches, we were seeing the power of God working in people's lives. There is no way of describing what that is like. One man in Kentucky owned the largest independent moving company in town. His wife said he was so mean their son had to move out of the house to keep from being beaten to death. He pulled his big Lincoln Continental into the parking lot of the church one day for a meeting and God changed that bear into a lamb. He brought scores of people to the meeting, many of whom received Christ as Saviour and Lord.

Once again, we had moved into our dream home in Naples. Once again, God was to move us out. Wally had done so well in school, they suggested he just skip the twelfth grade and enter college after the eleventh. When I dropped this sixteen-year-old lad off one day to take his ACT test, he kissed me on the cheek (a habit he still has at the age of 25), asked me to pray for him, tucked his red Bible under his arm and went in. When the results came back, he had scored in the 99th percentile—the highest

DEEP RIVER

score possible!

He obtained an academic scholarship at Tennessee Temple, making his plans to enter at sixteen. As I prayed about it, I began to form the conclusion that he was a bit young to shove out of the nest. Besides, Toy was suffering from the pressure at the school where she was attending, and I longed for my girls to have at least a couple of years in a private Christian school. After a lot of prayer, we began to load up our stuff and head north once again to Chattanooga. It was September, 1969. How strangely the river of grace runs!

> And he said unto me, Son of man, hast thou seen this? Then he brought me, and caused me to return to the brink of the river.
> Ezekiel 47:6

Chapter Fifteen

THE CHICKAMAUGA DAM has always reminded me of the grace of God. On one side, the shimmering waters of the lake back up to the blue-green Tennessee hills. It is a playground for the residents, affording numerous opportunities for boating, swimming, fishing, camping and exploring. It speaks of abundance and blessing. On the other side, the waters are much lower and treacherous as they rush away from the spillways of the hydroelectric generators. The lower waters can only receive as much as the huge valves of the spill gates will permit them to. In the same way, faith, the channel of God's grace, opens the way for Him to provide us with His abundant and inexhaustible blessings.

About two miles north of this place, our family was to spend years of healing and blessing. One of the lessons of our long journey is that if we can be true when our faith is being tested, an enlargement always lies ahead. He is simply trying to bring us into a large place, as the children of Israel discovered in their wanderings. After they had come to the waters of Marah and seen the bitter waters

DEEP RIVER

healed, the divine record says:

> And they came to Elim, where were twelve wells of water, and threescore and ten palm trees: and they encamped there by the waters.
> Exodus 15:27

The relationship of a pastor's family with a church is hard to understand unless you experience it yourself. You put your life, heart and soul, into the lives of a group of people. You hope for their best, weep when they fall, rejoice when they grow and bind your life to theirs in a thousand imperceptible ways. In Fort Myers, when we told our kids we were finally leaving our first pastorate, Joan and I had seen a dramatic example of the emotional involvement we share with a church. Our fifteen-year-old son had come to the side of our bed late one night, after all the pain and testing, to attempt to talk us into staying. It was an unforgettable scene.

"But what's going to happen to these people?"

"Son, God will send them someone else to love them and care for them."

"But nobody will love them the way we do!"

Our son stood by our bedside sobbing uncontrollably for some time. It was as if we were reaching into his heart and pulling it out by the roots. There was no consoling him. No pastor's family can really walk off and leave a congregation without literally leaving a part of themselves behind. We had made it a rule, however, never to discuss church problems or the shortcomings of other Christians in the presence of our children except in the most constructive terms. We did not want to be guilty of causing our kids to grow up bitter toward the church.

FIFTEEN

We had rented a duplex in Chattanooga down in a hollow off Germantown Road. We affectionately named it "the mole hole." I was preaching in meetings all over the country. One day I drove home from a meeting in Bay Minette, Alabama, to be greeted in the driveway by an excited Joan.

"I've found the house I want!" she declared.

"This means trouble," I groaned to myself.

I knew Joan. She would not want a nice house with everything finished and all the comforts. What she looked for in a house was a challenge (translated *work*, and lots of it, for me). Endowed with a gift of mercy, Joan has always loved animals. So I knew right away it meant a place in the country. (That meant lots of time and gasoline.) She preferred a place that was not sterile. What she wanted was something with character, uniqueness and flexibility. While I was quickly assessing what all this might mean, I could hardly guess what she had found.

I never would have dreamed it was as bad as it was.

The lady who had lived in the little house behind "W" Road Chapel was moving and Joan had made her an offer on her house. It was a two bedroom house with the drywall taped together with masking tape. The front entrance was ground level, but if you walked out the other door, you would fall straight down twelve feet! Perched on a slope of Signal Mountain, it looked like the houses in "Snuffy Smith." The outside was finished in tar paper. One room had the walls done in cardboard boxes. Doors led to the outside from every direction, but there were no porches.

When I looked at it, I just groaned. Joan was exuberant.

"I just want it for a little retreat! Buy it for me for my

birthday!"

The price was reasonable enough—$4,000, including the seven and a half acres of thickly forested mountain land. The owner was willing to sell it to us on time.

"You could pay that much for a car, and in a couple of years not have anything," Joan argued.

I groaned again. Her reasoning was devastating.

Upon inspection I noticed the house was built with solid oak timbers underneath, with an oak sub floor and tongue and groove hardwood flooring throughout. It was solid.

I looked around the grounds, which were paved with beer cans. Our reactions were a study in contrasts. Every time we would look at something, Joan would say, "Oooh!"

I would say, "Ohhhh . . . !"

But overhead, towering hardwood trees provided a haven for songbirds and scampering squirrels. We could look out and see a breathtaking view of the City of Chattanooga, and beyond it, the foothills of the Smokies on that clear day. Wildflowers peered above the underbrush, sprinkling the surrounding woods with a patchwork of gorgeous color, and the smell of roses wafted from the huge rosebush in front of the house.

I knew I was fighting a losing battle. Little did I know I had just selected the homesite where I would finish rearing my family.

Joan's down-to-earth business sense was right on target. It has not only proven a good place to raise kids away from the distracting influence of an urban neighborhood, but it has also been a place of inspiration for me to deepen my theology and develop two of my great loves—art and writing. Patching the place up and remodeling it has proven a useful family project, welding

FIFTEEN

us together in a common improvement of the home environment. Kids need chores to do, and there have been chores aplenty here.

There's no telling how many times Joan had to firmly resist my desire to forsake this rustic little house and move into a big, fine home. The trouble is, I probably would have been just as restless in any home. I have desperately needed the character development that comes through learning to be content, letting some roots sink in and facing the responsibility of staying by the stuff. How I pray that God will give Joan and me the grace to instill a sense of security and staying power in the lives of our kids! And how encouraging to learn that when God chooses your lifetime partner, He brings together just the right ingredients so that each can see the blind spots and minister to the needs of the other.

After spending Christmas day in Kent, Ohio, with Aunt Rose, we drove through snow all the way back to Chattanooga. The four inches of snow that fell on the town literally crippled it. These southern cities cannot afford to invest in the equipment necessary to clear huge amounts of snow, since the snowfalls are so scarce. I was scheduled to speak at a little church meeting in a schoolhouse in Hixson, a suburb of Chattanooga, but I couldn't get our big sedan out of "the mole hole."

Jim Williams, our good friend with whom we were sharing the duplex, loaned me his little Volkswagen "beetle," and we drove north across the Chickamauga Dam to where twenty-five people had managed to come to the services that morning.

They looked lost in the large cafetorium of the Hixson Elementary School. We met on the stage. In struggling to get the car out of the drive, I had burst the collar button on my shirt and the clip-on tie I was wearing would not

DEEP RIVER

stay on. Those warm, friendly people did not seem to care when I simply discarded it and went on to teach a Sunday School lesson and deliver the morning message. They were a compatible crowd. Staunch, middle-class Tennesseans, many of them had moved here years ago to work in the factories and plants of Chattanooga. They gave off an aura of quiet, settled concern and the "I know where I'm going" kind of attitude.

After this service, one of the men called me to ask if I would be interested in taking this church. There was more involved than just the fact that I liked the people and saw a challenge to build another work. Having been in a traveling ministry for over a year now, I was beginning to see a need to spend more quality time with my children, especially the girls during this important period of their lives. And you could easily fool Joan. She never really identified with the ministry of any preacher except the one she married. She was really not happy under the ministry of other pastors.

I met with their pulpit committee one Sunday afternoon. I fell in love with these three men, Elbert Kilgore, Clyde Cox and Wib Welton. They questioned me about my doctrine and I asked them questions about their church. I learned that they had also experienced deep waters of trial. A moral situation had developed in the church involving three of the leading families, and the ensuing disturbance had ripped the small congregation apart. They needed somebody to love them. We needed somebody to love us. It was an ideal wedding.

As I left that meeting that Sunday afternoon, I thought I could hear the hills singing as the brilliant Tennessee sun dipped down in the West. Lake Chickamauga was painted a brilliant gold, and the sky glowed with excitement. On the car radio, a Christian station was broad-

FIFTEEN

casting one of my favorite hymns, and my heart was filled with joy. Whether that was the peace of God concerning my decision, I don't know. I do know it was the foreshadowing of the way this congregation was to take my family into its bosom and love us with a fervent love, bringing beauty out of the ashes of testing.

After we had prayed about it as a family, the official call came Sunday, January 29, in the evening. After acknowledging to Elbert Kilgore that I would accept, I met Monday morning with a building contractor and then with a church bond director, starting the wheels rolling on a building program. We have hardly stopped since, in all of these eight years.

Not that I haven't felt that old restlessness several times. I sometimes think a preacher is like Abraham, never knowing what town he will be in next. Pastoring is hard, gruelling work. The whole family is on call twenty-four hours a day. It is very seldom that a church member will call up to share a blessing, although it does occasionally happen. When they call, it is usually during the worst of circumstances, when they have tried to work out their problems and failed. So the conscientious pastor's work is not only that of overcoming the natural reluctance of people to become involved in spiritual things, but of sharing the burdens of their most difficult circumstances. Unlike the doctor or lawyer, who operates best when professionally detached, the minister of the gospel cannot detach himself from the burden and needs of his people. Their burdens become his burdens, and burden after burden falls upon his willing shoulders.

Nor is that the most important function. I have come to believe that one of the most important roles of the pastor is to provide a living model. In applying Bible truths and principles to his own personal life and that of

DEEP RIVER

his family, the congregation sees that these things are real. They work. For if they can work in the honest, transparent environment of the home, they can work anywhere. It is not in a pew for an hour on Sunday morning when the true character of faith is tested, but in the constant press of responsibility, the life-in-the-raw that takes place when family members live together in the common struggle to survive.

Too many people see a caricature of Christianity. They see a superficial, polished-halo kind of thing that only works on Sunday morning. But the vital truths of the living Word of God wear far more rugged shoes than that. Jesus Christ can meet the need of broken hearts, broken relationships, physical stress and jarring conflict. The Saviour who came to reconcile erring man to a just God can reconcile any two people.

Jesus Christ does not confine his work to a "sanctuary" where a few dozen people come together for a "religious break," like a coffee break. He works in the kitchen, in the garage, in the playroom and the marketplace.

Every life has a message. For good or bad, a life speaks. All of the testings, the forging, the molding in our lives were shaping us into a message for the people who would come into contact with our lives.

The Christian who shrinks from trial is shirking the very mold by which his Lord wants to shape his particular message for the hearts of a hungry world. To the Christian—not in his ivory palaces of superficial Sunday morning experience, but in the fires of life—the world is still saying, "Sirs, we would see Jesus!"

> And there shall be upon every high mountain, and upon every high hill, rivers and streams of waters in the day of the great slaughter, when the towers fall.
> Isaiah 30:25

Chapter Sixteen

SUCK CREEK is the torrent that rushes along the "Grand Canyon of Tennessee," the gorge that separates Mount Aetna and Signal Mountain. Here, at Signal Point, a beautiful little state park, Wally and Katie were to one day exchange their wedding vows on the edge of spacious splendor. But for now, a new adventure lay ahead of him.

Wally was spending the summer in the French Alps as a summer missionary. On the trail where Napoleon's troops bivouacked years before, he and his team of young companions were restoring an ancient building to use as a camp for French young people. My father was using his bed, once again having come to Chattanooga to spend some time with us.

One Sunday morning, the alarm clock jarred me loose from my bed at four o'clock. Part of our plan for teaching our girls responsibility was for them to have an afternoon paper route, which meant that one of us had to do the driving for them every day. While Joan did it most of the time, we took turns for the Sunday paper, which was delivered in the morning. Today was my turn. I stood for a couple of minutes staring blankly into the closet, wondering what one wears at four o'clock on Sunday morning.

As I took in my first transfusion of coffee a few minutes later, Dad appeared at the kitchen door. We sleepily exchanged greetings and he drifted back into the bedroom. We didn't know that many anxious hours lay just ahead.

A slight, stooped man with flaming red hair, Dad's face bore the unmistakable impress of the outdoors, like a weathered old board. Freckles scattered themselves nonchalantly across his face and arms, which were also spotted occasionally with sun cancers. His huge, calloused hands revealed the honorable badge of the working man.

By now, alcohol had robbed him of almost everything in his life. He had become completely dependent upon others. Vascular disease had made necessary vein transplants in his legs. His digestive system was gone, and the drugs frequently given to him in the veterans' hospitals only made him more dependent.

The morning light had just begun to turn the trees from black to silver-grey that morning as we made our way back up "W" Road to the side of Signal Mountain. Remembering the hard day that lay ahead, I yielded to the temptation to catch an additional few winks on the couch. A scant half-hour later the house came alive with the usual Sunday morning preparation.

I checked Dad's room to see if he felt well enough to attend the services. It was empty. A check of the rest of the house revealed that he was nowhere to be found. I walked out onto the deck that protruded over the mountain slope, calling for him. The whole worried household

SIXTEEN

began to scout the premises.

It was three miles to the nearest place of business at the bottom of the mountain, and about the same distance to any store at the top. Our house was situated 400 feet below the highway that makes four hairpin curves on its way to the top of the mountain. Thick, heavily wooded slopes stretch 4,000 feet below our house before they touch Mountain Creek Road at the bottom. It was not a very healthy place for a half-invalid to wander off. We searched the surrounding woods for some time before I decided to call the county police.

Deputies were combing the area and an all-points bulletin had been broadcast before I was persuaded to go on to church. During the course of the morning's activities we called the police frequently, only to learn that no clues had been found to Dad's whereabouts. Upon returning home we learned that two men on the rescue squad had walked the distance of the woods to the bottom of the slope. Patrol cars had searched "W" Road from top to bottom. Still nothing.

Pictures of Dad lying somewhere in the woods, hurt and needing help, would not leave my mind. In a normal location, the situation would not have seemed so dangerous. But from here, I knew he was in trouble.

Hours dragged by without any word. The daylight continued to offer some hope, but nightfall shrouded my heart with despair. He was so physically helpless that a child would have a better chance in those woods at night. Every imaginable possibility tried to push itself into my mind. Sleep simply could not overcome the pounding of my anxious heart.

The next day was just minutes old when I started my own walk down the slope with a friend, but we failed to find any sign of him. Checks with law enforcement agen-

DEEP RIVER

cies continued to reveal nothing. Inquiries at homes and businesses were fruitless. Several "leads" fizzled. Hope waned.

In mid-afternoon the phone brought the first news. A city policeman had turned up an unidentified character on Mountain Creek Road. In a few minutes I found myself peering through the window of a police cruiser at the foot of "W" Road.

"Can you take me to where my son lives?" the almost unrecognizable man in the back seat asked.

It was Dad, all right, but he didn't recognize me. The officer said he had found him crouched before a fence near the roadside, reaching through the wire and pulling the leaves from the other side, mumbling something about money. I began to put together what must have happened. His mind had simply blanked out, and he had wandered through the woods. Only these woods were not like his beloved Florida woods, and the force of gravity had rammed his frail body across every jutting rock and into every tree in his path for 4,000 feet.

He was a mass of bruises and wounded flesh. There was hardly a place on his body that did not display a bruise. His face was swollen and bleeding, and his red hair was matted and full of burrs. He was mumbling incoherently about "working on the railroad with my daddy," and about how "some boy stole my wallet." He had obviously lost his wallet containing his small government check.

As we drove back to the house I wondered about the noxious disease he had lived with for so long. I had seen it rob him of his manhood. It had killed his career and destroyed his self-respect. I fought back tears as I remembered how he had taught me the craft that enabled me to save thousands of dollars for the congregations I

SIXTEEN

served. Over the years his children had watched this disease destroy his usefulness and reduce him to a childish babbler. But this is not a disease resulting from an accident or a germ. It is a disease legally sold in bottles and cans, and from which a mammoth industry profits handsomely.

I am the first to admit that a man makes the choice himself to drink or not to drink. But as we poured peroxide on a hundred cuts and bruises, one throbbing question wracked my mind: "How *could* they? How could *anybody*? How could anybody consciously, for profit, manufacture a product designed for the systematic destruction of the human mind? And what kind of society, what kind of morality would perpetuate its respectability and legalize its deadliness? Why does the victim waste away in jails and hospitals while the profiteer sits in the seat of power and respect?

As I pulled off Dad's trousers to bathe his legs, he reached into his pocket and pulled out a handful of dead leaves. "Take good care of this gold," he said. "I found it by the railroad."

We decided not to take him to the hospital and get him started on drugs again. He recovered his reason in a couple of days. But the incident left a profound effect upon me. One individual is worth more, Jesus said, than the whole world. How many times had this kind of tragedy been enacted over and over again? How many individuals and their families were affected by this plague? In 1973 Americans emptied enough barrels of beer to stretch 70,000 miles. How many of these human derelicts had been made by that deep, treacherous river?

Fearing another incident of the sort, and because of our demanding, rigorous schedule, it was necessary to put him on an airplane back to Florida. We made ar-

DEEP RIVER

rangements for wheelchairs to be provided at every stop. None of us in the family could afford the kind of care he needed. It was the last time I would see my father alive.

The following January Joan, Wally and I attended a conference on the family. Through a searching study of the Scriptures I learned that many of the things affecting my decisions and behavior were linked to my youth. But God's grace is more than sufficient to make up the difference. We pledged to one another that we would work harder to build the kind of lasting values our future generations would profit from.

Berean Baptist Church had grown steadily into a flourishing congregation. Berean Academy, planned and conceived to provide a quality Christian education, had joined the number of private church schools springing up across the nation. But I was beginning to be consumed with a holy war against alcohol.

Early one Sunday morning, I was jarred from my sleep once again, this time by the telephone. Dad had succumbed in his sleep. I called John Innes, my assistant pastor, and made arrangements for him to conduct the Sunday services, while I made my way south from airport to airport by standby reservation. It was December 24, 1973.

> Rivers of waters run down mine eyes, because they keep not thy law.
> Psalm 119:136

Chapter Seventeen

NOT TOO FAR from Naples Memorial Gardens, Clam Pass runs out to the Gulf. It was near the kind of place that he loved, where mullet run in schools and the smell of salt water drifts across a marsh grass flat, that we buried my father's body.

The day after Christmas, at two in the afternoon, the funeral director pulled the family room curtains closed, and I gathered my sisters and brothers around the coffin for a final word of prayer. I walked out of the family room, around into the front of the chapel and down the aisle to the rostrum. There, I conducted Dad's memorial service myself at my own request. Among other things, I told them that I loved him.

There was no inheritance to fight over. He left behind a wristwatch, a shoe box full of photographs and an empty wallet. I personally think he was more a victim than a villain.

If I hated liquor before, I hated it with a passion after his death. It was not as much a sense of personal tragedy as something else. I did not feel cheated in life, or even that Dad's tragic life was any more tragic than any other unfortunate life. What was happening was that the more I investigated the problem, the more Dad's case became a symbol of a thing of monstrous proportions.

Watergate had already torn the nation apart. Frankly, I could not see the sense of great tragedy involved in a few Republican burglars breaking into the Democratic national headquarters. But it was a tragedy to the devotees of statism and government service. Charles Colson, in his search for meaning in his life, ran into the statement that helped turn his life around in *Mere Christianity* by C. S. Lewis:

> And immorality makes this other difference, which, by the by, had a connection with the difference between totalitarianism and democracy. If individuals live only seventy years, then a state, or a nation, or a civilisation, which may last for a thousand years, is more important than an individual. But if Christianity is true, then the individual is not only more important but incomparably more important, for he is everlasting and the life of a state or a civilisation, compared with his, is only a moment.

We had voted in liquor-by-the-drink in Chattanooga, and the main argument was that the community needed the extra taxes. Then I would go down to skid row and work with the empty hulks of men down there and wonder if all the taxes in the world were worth what alcohol did to one individual. But in researching the alcohol problem, I learned that even that was a lie. According to Federal reports, the total annual tax revenue

SEVENTEEN

from alcohol—federal, state and local—was eight billion dollars. According to the HEW, "alcohol abuse" costs the nation twenty-five billion annually. That's seventy million per day. Even subtracting the tax revenue, it leaves a dead loss to the country of seventeen million. That's over four dollars loss to every head of household in the country every week!

I sent off to the Justice Department for figures on alcohol and crime. A 1973 study showed that 43 percent of all arrests in the country were for alcohol offenses alone! That's almost half the nation's court case load. But it by no means tells the full effect upon the nation's courts. These are only offenses like drunk driving, liquor law violations, etc. Other cases such as aggravated assault, murder and other violent crimes show that more than half of them are alcohol-related. In other words, more than half the policemen, jails and judges in the United States are there just to keep the alcohol interests in business.

I talked to a hospital official who told me he thought half the hospital admissions in the country were alcohol-related.

I asked a case worker for the welfare department who worked almost exclusively with child abuse cases what percentage of them resulted from the parents being intoxicated. His answer was shocking: "Every single one, almost without exception. If it is not a case of mental retardation or insanity, you can almost be sure it's alcohol or drugs."

In nearby Cleveland, Tennessee, nationwide attention was recently focused on the case of five-year-old Melissha Gibson, who was fed hot sauce, made to walk continuously and abused until she died. "Child abuse" was the cry that filled the air. Testimony was brought out in the parents' trial which showed that her stepfather was allegedly drinking throughout the duration of this incident and every other time Melissha suffered abuse. Yet the press mentioned almost nothing about the possibility of alcohol as a contributing factor.

I was also moved by the terrible tragedy of child abuse, but I could not help but wonder how many fewer cases there would be if parents did not succumb to the numbing, inhibition-destroying effects of alcohol.

I began to study volumes on the problem, discovering that one area of the subject is absolutely taboo. Any mention of the possibility of controlling or reducing sale or consumption of alcohol is met with disdain. It is not alcohol that is the problem. It is something else, some strange chemistry in the victim's personality or an element in the environment. Consumed with the vastness of the problem, that seems to me to be the biggest lie that has ever been told.

Apathy to the problem was so evident I did not know how to do anything about it. I knew I couldn't make it a "hobby horse" in my ministry, preaching about it all the time. I had an obligation to feed my people, and to preach the whole counsel of God. The idea occurred to me to try to get something published.

I wrote and submitted a number of articles to Christian publications. While some of them were sympathetic to the problem, they did not feel the subject was appropriate for publication, explaining that the war had already been fought and lost. Some of them wrote back and said the only answer was to "get them saved."

Secular book publishers were not interested in the queries sent to them. *The Reader's Digest* expressed compassionate interest in a first person article, but said they could not fit it in. The more I studied the problem, the

SEVENTEEN

more enormous it became. I would fly into a rage every time I passed a huge liquor sign. The whole frustrating picture was tearing away at my insides. I simply could not accept the incredible fact that such apathy to this criminal problem existed.

Our young people had rioted in the streets over Vietnam. But in all the years of that deadliest and costliest of wars, 55,000 Americans died. Alcohol kills four times that many every year! I could not imagine if somebody dropped a bomb on the United States each year that killed that many people, we would issue the bomber a license.

The FDA was banning products right and left, even telling poor Euel Gibbons he could no longer talk about eating pine trees. But there was no proof that most of these products had ever harmed a single human being. Ralph Nader had almost singlehandedly depressed the automobile industry with his demands for safer cars, but he had not said a word about the intoxicated drivers who kill more than 25,000 people a year on the nation's highways.

It is dangerous to get into such a thing. There is something about the mind that has to put things into a reasonable pattern. When reality no longer can be reasoned out, the mind recoils. I was staggering under the sheer enormity of it.

During a revival meeting I was preaching in Baltimore, I interviewed a crack investigative reporter for the now defunct *National Observer* in their Washington office. I had talked to him before and had followed some of his crusading journalism, taking up the cause of unfortunate individuals. He was courteous and accommodating, but he could not identify with the problem. I told him I thought the only answer was for somebody to focus at-

DEEP RIVER

tention on the fact that the industry was responsible for the problem, and had to somehow assume the financial responsibility. If even only to the extent that manufacturers would be responsible for the harm wrought through their products.

"I think it is a man's business if he wants to drink or sell it," he said.

"But you just got through telling me that you thought industry ought to be penalized for polluting the water, and that all guns ought to be controlled," I protested.

His next statement was almost unbelievable.

"I just can't see where alcohol does that much harm most of the time," he said.

It was too much. I could not accept the fact that an intelligent, compassionate individual could be so blind to a problem of such massive proportions.

At a Baltimore radio station the next morning I was scheduled to give a thirty minute live talk on alcohol. Standing in the waiting room, I saw the place start swimming and blacked out. After a few minutes, I was able to go ahead with the broadcast. But as I closed the service that night, a terrible pain rose up first in the abdomen, then my side. With the heads of the congregation bowed, I called on the pastor to close in prayer and I staggered out the side door of the church and made my way to the adjacent pastorium and collapsed, writhing in pain.

Two nights later in Chattanooga, I paced the floor in pain. Joan called the doctor, who made arrangements to put me in the hospital. Two surgeries within six weeks with a few days in the intensive care unit followed. Except for tests, I had never been a patient in a hospital before, but I spent a month in two different hospitals, letting time and treatment take its course.

> His eyes are as the eyes of doves
> by the rivers of waters, washed
> with milk, and fitly set.
> Song of Solomon 5:12

Chapter Eighteen

I COULDN'T SEE the Tennessee River through the faded curtains which framed the dingy hospital room in the old Newell Hospital, soon to be torn down and replaced with another. Besides the aging Krystal Restaurant on the corner, several blocks of downtown buildings lay between the hospital and where the historic old river wound its way around Moccasin Bend.

As the day wore on, thirty-three visitors made their way into the small room. My love for people was wearing thin. I knew they were coming to comfort me, but most of them inevitably got around to talking about their problems, a natural inclination when you're talking to your pastor. In my depleted condition, I was wishing they would just go away and leave me alone. I was weak, tired and depressed.

It was hard to indulge that luxury. I was telling myself, "Preachers can get weak and depressed. Even the great ones like Jonah, Moses and Elijah." A couple more called on the telephone, tacitly getting around to bringing me up to date on their problems. I screamed on the inside

DEEP RIVER

while trying to remain calm on the outside. I was hurting, crushed, retreating. It was the third day after the second surgery and I had just been released from the intensive care unit. Even after the other things had been corrected by surgery, I was still suffering from hepatitis and an ulcer.

In the terrible weakness of those days, I was reeling from the problems. I had waged a hopeless fight that accomplished nothing. The church had been caught in the rapid rise of building costs while building an educational building, then in the crush of the recession of '74. For the first time in memory, churches across the land had gone bankrupt. In struggling with our financial crisis, attention had been diverted away from the kind of things that stimulate growth, and the church had stood virtually still for a couple of years.

That night was probably the worst night of my life. Horrible nightmares of things rushing at me jarred me loose each time I dozed off. With blurring speed and crushing force, every conceivable kind of creature and thing was stampeding through my mind. The drugs didn't do any good. I was afraid to close my eyes anymore. I prayed constantly that I might retain my sanity.

The next morning I awoke from a fitful nap to see Joan leaning over me. She held a small, folded card out to me with a rose on the front. On the inside, she had carefully copied a poem we had in our scrapbook:

> Come! Grow old along with me!
>   The best is yet to be.
> Our times are in His hand
>   Who saith, "A whole I planned."
> Youth shows but half; trust God.
>   See all, nor be afraid.

EIGHTEEN

Dear, sweet Joan. I know she had to get a special strength from the Lord during this time. Her confidence that God was in this, too, had great healing for me. It had been like that. At times I had to be her strength. At other times, she was used of God to minister to me. How perfectly God works out His plan for our lives.

That boost for my spirits was helped by the fact that the good people of our church rallied to our side to help meet the medical costs. Hundreds of dollars were provided by loving hands to meet the need.

I received word that my book on suffering had been accepted for publication. God was fitting all the pieces of His great plan together. The deep river of grace was sweeping through our lives, giving great cause for thanksgiving and praise. One thing was for sure: From now on I could have a lot more compassion when I visited people in the hospital!

As a greater realization of God's grace began to creep over me, I won some new victories. One of them was to come to grips with some things the Great Surgeon wanted to weed out of my life. In all of this, the awful picture I had seen of a gruesome alcohol problem had etched my heart with a certain amount of bitterness. I came to realize I couldn't have written responsibly about the problem even if somebody had been willing to listen. I was too emotionally involved. Amy Young, an Accent Books author, told me months later that when a person is so caught up in a situation emotionally, he loses his objectivity. And editors, of all people, can spot that easily.

In my preaching at the rescue mission, I had spoken with a vengeance. I was telling myself I had to get the attention of these hardened, alcohol-saturated people. But in reality, I suppose, I was preaching out of my hatred of everything alcohol stood for. (I hope I don't lose that hatred. I still think it is a problem of huge magnitude.)

I decided one night to preach to the men on forgiveness and love. As I studied the subject, a strange realization came over me. In all this, I had almost totally ignored my mother! Oh, I had extended all the usual courtesies and told her I loved her, but it dawned on me that I was identifying her with the alcohol problem because I was associating it with my former home life. If all this sounds like some Freudian hangup, it wasn't. The Lord simply reminded me through the Scriptures that I had not been expressive and outgoing in my love for her.

I didn't feel I could deliver that message to those men that night until I had made the thing right. I called her long distance, asking her forgiveness. While she listened in flabbergasted protest, I told her I had not been right in my attitude toward her, and had not shown the love a son is supposed to show his mother. I managed to get a faltering offer of forgiveness from her and felt much better. I think our relationship has been better since then.

But the Heavenly Surgeon was not through. The time came when my conscience would give me no rest until I called Joan's dad and asked his forgiveness for running off and marrying her against his wishes (we had been married for almost 25 years!). He accepted my apology graciously, and I was gratified. He had made much of his money in the business I detested, but I had wronged him, violated his authority over his own daughter and had been unforgiving in my attitude toward him.

Other similar incidents followed. It is one thing to recognize and fight a terrible, consuming terror like alcohol. It is quite another thing to hold bitterness in one's heart against another human being.

I am sure that when God looked at me, my sins looked as black and terrible as anybody's sins. Whatever any

EIGHTEEN

other man has done, it took just as much of the grace of God to forgive me as it did him. Furthermore, there is enough of it to go around. There is no limit to God's ability to reach out in mercy and cleanse a man or woman, no matter how dark their lives.

> Come now, and let us reason together, saith the Lord: though your sins be as scarlet, they shall be as white as snow; though they be red like crimson, they shall be as wool.
> Isaiah 1:18

I long for the day when somebody can do something about alcohol in this country. My research and experiences have convinced me that the manufacturers and sellers of alcohol should be no more exempt for the harm brought by their product than any other manufacturer. If they were in some way held responsible, many of them would not be so willing to profit from the unspeakable suffering of others.

If drinkers had to be licensed as drivers are licensed, perhaps deaths would be reduced and the problem would decline. If a person could be shown to be one of the ten million problem drinkers in this country, his privileges could be revoked for his own good and his family's relief. Should a dealer continue to sell to a drinker whose license was revoked, he could be liable for a damage suit.

I know this may seem like a far-fetched idea, but it is merely one of dozens of alternatives that could be applied to the problem to control its disastrous results. It has been convincingly demonstrated that the problem will never be solved by simply treating the unhappy, already addicted victims. Somehow, the problem will have to be dealt with at the source. The U.S. government once spent

DEEP RIVER

over two million dollars to find out what causes alcoholism! It shows the tremendous blind spot that exists about the problem on every level.

Churches and agencies must realize the problem is not something that is just old hat or a dead issue—something we have come to accept and are willing to live with. It is very much alive, and requires tremendous dedication to correct its ravages.

But I have learned that, while alcohol is a rushing torrent of disaster, the river of God's grace is greater. "Where sin did abound, grace did much more abound." There is healing, marvelous and complete, for anybody who will put his trust in Jesus Christ.

For twenty-nine years now that spiritual river has flowed in my life. Since I went to the Fountain, I have not wanted for satisfaction nor had a thirst unfulfilled. All of the things men do to satisfy their longing—their craving for a thing that lies always beyond their reach—can be satisfied by the One who told the woman at the well:

> Whosoever drinketh of this water shall thirst again: But whosoever drinketh of the water that I shall give him shall never thirst; but the water that I shall give him shall be in him a well of water springing up into everlasting life.
> John 4:13,14